WINNERS AND LOSERS

BRIAN BLANDFORD

A Division of GL Publications
Ventura, California, U.S.A.

Rights for publishing this book in other languages are contracted by Gospel Literature International foundation (GLINT). GLINT also provides technical help for the adaptation, translation, and publishing of Bible study resources and books in over 100 languages worldwide. For further information, contact GLINT, Post Office Box 6688, Ventura, California 93006, U.S.A., or the publisher.

Scripture quotations in this publication are from *The New International Version*, Holy Bible. Copyright © 1978 by New York International Bible Society. Used by permission.
Quotation from Derek Prince's *Faith to Live By*, copyright 1977 by Derek Prince, published by Servant Books, Ann Arbor, Michigan, and CGM Publishing, Fort Lauderdale, Florida.

© Copyright 1985 by Regal Books
Published by Regal Books
A Division of GL Publications
Ventura, California 93006
Printed in U.S.A.

Library of Congress Cataloging in Publication Data.
Blandford, Brian, 1937-
   Winners and losers.

   Summary: Two leaders of a church youth group discuss parallels between Biblical characters and members of their group.
    [1. Christian life—Fiction]   I. Title.
PZ7.B6115Wi   1985   [Fic]   84-26709
ISBN 0-8307-1012-4

Acknowledgements

Thanks . . .

to my wife Mair and my sons Simon, Matthew, Philip, and Richard, for being willing to see even less of me than usual whilst this book was in the making;

to Bruce and Phyllis Macartney for kindly letting me retreat to their idyllic New Forest cottage to complete the project;

to Jean Calais for her skill and happy tolerance in transforming my terrible writing into a typed manuscript;

to Rick Bundschuh, youth editor of Gospel Light, without whose friendship and encouragement this would never have been written.

Prologue

Hi! Welcome to Fairmont.

Where is Fairmont, you ask? Well, my geography isn't too good, so we'll just have to say it's in America, somewhere. Or, on the other hand, anywhere.

I want you to meet the most unusual bunch of kids. They belong to the youth group at Fairmont Community Church, and what their long-suffering youth pastor thinks of them is nobody's business. No, that's not quite true. It's his, and the guy who's taking over his job, and—oh, you'll soon find out all about it.

One more thing. You're not just going to eavesdrop on this mixed bag of young men and women. You'll be brushing with some pretty powerful characters from the Bible too. In fact, to make sense of the whole thing, you're going to need your Bible right alongside this little book.

Ready? OK—walk with me down Main Street, Fairmont and . . . yes, this looks like the place. Come on in.

Chapter 1

"Why," sighed Bill Pulkington to himself, "do things that came out of boxes never fit when you put them back in?"

For the fifth time he pulled his stereo out of the carton and unwrapped the cords to try a different way. He looked gloomily around his apartment. Boxes stood everywhere, bulging and spilling, the result of 10 years of random acquisition of the useful, the useless, the decorative and the ugly, the implements and the impediments of bachelor life. The place looked like a downtown junk shop.

Bill tried another halfhearted push to force the reluctant carton to swallow the stereo, thought better of it, and sat down on the one corner of the bed that was not covered with clothes, books, or tennis rackets. His thoughts wandered over the 10 years he had spent as youth pastor of Fairmont Community Church—10 happy, infuriating, exciting, depressing, lovely, frustrating, satisfying years. He thought of the teenagers he'd seen grow into adults and the children who had become his present set of teens. What a bunch! He shook his head ruefully as some of the faces imaged themselves in his mind. No doubt about it; on the whole it had been a good time, but now it was moving-on time. A few days more and this chapter in his life would be closed . . .

A loud buzz disturbed his musings. He moved across to the security phone. "Yes?"

"It's Mike," crackled a voice from the speaker.

"Sure, come on up." Bill pressed the button to release the electronic lock at the front of the apartment building and after a minute or two a light rapping on his door announced the arrival of his visitor.

Mike Baldwin was to take over for Bill at Fairmont. They had already gotten together over the last couple of weeks, and with the true pastor's concern Bill was anxious to share as much information as he could to help Mike build on the foundation laid in a decade of hard, exhausting work.

As the tall, blond Englishman came in, Bill flashed a quick but genuine welcoming smile at him, "Excuse the mess. I'm in the middle of packing."

"I would never have guessed," mocked Mike good-humoredly. "Say, if it's inconvenient, we can leave it."

"No, no, it's fine. Look, I've got something special I want to go over with you these last three nights. Behold!"

Bill made an elaborate flourish with his hands towards a corner of the room—like a conjuror about to show his greatest illusion. There Mike saw a superb computer, complete with disk drives, monitor, and printer.

Mike whistled, "Whew! What a beaut!"

"A hobby of mine," explained Bill. "I use it for all my records, which is why I'm showing it to you. Before I pack it away I want to run through my special confidential file. I'll do a printout of the whole thing for you to keep. I'd like you to get to know some of the kids I've had. Some of them have left, some you'll be taking over."

"That's great," Mike responded warmly. "It'll be a tremendous help just to have some background."

"I hope so. But there's more to it than that. You see, I have a theory that everyone who ever lived will find themselves mirrored in the Bible, not just in a general way but in the characters that populate its pages. I think we've all got a spiritual and temperamental double somewhere between these covers."

He tapped the Bible that Mike was holding in his hand. "So

what I've done on my computer file is to put a few outline remarks about each particular kid, and then I just think about where I've met him or her before in the Bible. Then I add a couple of code letters to remind me."

"Sounds fun," said Mike.

"It's more than fun. I find it helps me understand why the kids act the way they do. It's a tremendous help in caring for them pastorally. I know more about them than they know about themselves because God has shown me in His Word what really makes them tick."

"Mind you," he continued, "I'm not always right."

Mike warmed to the modesty of the man.

"But it's fascinating how many times when I've identified a guy or a girl with someone in the Bible how often that one will run true-to-type as events and circumstances work out. The winners follow the winners and the losers are the losers time after time after time."

"Sounds a bit fatalistic."

"Not a bit of it—because God has given us the opportunity for change, as I hope you will see."

"OK, well, I'm bursting to start."

"Sure—pull up a chair or a box or something. I've loaded the machine. We're all set. Let's go."

Chapter 2

The two youth leaders hunched around the monitor and Bill began punching the keys. A screenful of letters flashed on the screen, displaying the main menu of Bill's program. His fingers hovered over the keyboard.

"Now you choose. Would you like to start with a winner or a loser?"

"Well, remembering how my mother always said, 'Eat your cabbage first and then you can have your ice cream,' I think I'll plump for a loser."

"OK, let's see. Let's try this guy." Bill's dexterous touch made rapid clicks and the tube rolled up a page of dense print. Mike read out loud! "Kurt Neilsen: Age 19. Address: 1560 Mattan Avenue. Tel: 555-3140."

The name at this stage meant nothing to him and he was already scanning the next section with the simple heading "Comments." He carried on reading aloud.

"Problem guy. Too rich, too powerful, too pig-headed. Few friends; trial to the group. Needs God's discipline."

Mike shrugged his shoulders. "Sounds like he can't be a Christian. And it also sounds like you're being a bit judgmental."

"It's true, Kurt's not a Christian. And I admit what I've put there sounds like I'm jumping on him. But I haven't told the half.

Those comments of mine are only a skeleton of truth so I can pray realistically for him. But I really fear for his soul. You see my Bible code letters down the bottom there?"

Mike noticed a *Ph* standing on its own.

"That stands for Pharaoh. To me, Kurt is a real modern-day counterpart to that monster Moses had to deal with way back in Exodus. Let's have a cup of coffee while I fill you in a bit on the background and my thinking about the guy."

Bill moved off his chair and hacked a path through the jungle undergrowth of his half-packed stuff to the coffee percolator on the far side of the room. As he busied himself getting the old machine into operation he carried on talking.

"I don't really know why Kurt ever came to us in the first place. He's not only *not* a Christian—he's positively *anti*. I think he may have started coming a couple of years ago because he had his eye on one of our girls—not that any of our girls have ever gone out with him."

Bill noticed Mike looking a bit troubled.

"Don't get me wrong," Bill continued. "The group didn't reject him. In fact they've been very gracious to him. It's Kurt's own fault. He seems to go out of his way to oppose everything we stand for. His heart is as hard as this coffee mug." Bill knocked the mug on the table to emphasize his point.

"I'll start at the beginning: Kurt comes from a very rich family that holds quite a bit of property in this town. In fact, the new youth wing I showed you yesterday is built on land we bought from Kurt's dad."

"So Kurt can't be all bad then; he's been pretty useful to you."

"You must be joking!" Mike was surprised at the scorn in Bill's voice. "The hassle we had! The arguments over legal rights, money, everything. It was just about the time that Kurt began to come to the group. Far from being a bridge to help us get across the divide, he seemed to be digging the gulf wider."

Mike chipped in. "Is that your Pharaoh tie-up? Instead of 'let my people go' it's 'let my land go so I can have a youth wing'?" This time it was Mike who had scorn in his voice.

Bill brought over the two steaming mugs of coffee and a

sugar bowl, sat down, and pushed one mug and the sugar bowl towards Mike.

"No, of course it's not just that, though the parallel didn't escape me. It's Kurt's whole attitude. He seems determined to take on the power of God just like Pharaoh did, and the thing that I've had to observe and wonder about over the last few years is the way the Lord seems to be taking Kurt seriously. I know we've got to be careful in saying that events are God's direct intervention, but some strange things have happened to Kurt that make me think God is trying to say something. The trouble is, Kurt, like Pharaoh, seems deaf."

By now, for all his instinctive defense of the unknown Kurt, Mike knew that Bill was not making slick judgments but was speaking out of a lot of heart-searching and heartache.

"I think," said Bill as he stirred his coffee, "it would be good just to have a look at Pharaoh again. Got your Bible?"

Mike nodded.

"Well, let's start at that first confrontation between Moses and Pharaoh in Exodus 5."

Mike opened his Bible and leafed his way to the passage.

"You know," Bill mused as he waited for Mike to find the place, "it strikes me how there are no new problems under the sun. Pharaoh was bothered by exactly what bothers some governments today—not wanting to be swamped by immigrants and yet wanting to keep a supply of cheap labor. Anyway, we won't go into that now. It's Pharaoh's reply to Moses' demand for an exit visa that's important. Got verse 2 there?"

"OK . . . 'Who is the Lord, that I should obey him and let Israel go? I do not know the Lord and I will not let Israel go.'"

"Right," said Bill "and that was exactly Kurt's attitude over that land. When the hassle was beginning to get really sticky and all sorts of yucky letters were flying between the church board and Kurt's dad, we said to Kurt, 'Hey, couldn't you just have a chat with your dad and put in a good word for us?' You know what he said? He said, 'That's my business you're talking about—I'm going to inherit that one day. It's in my interest for it to make all the money possible.'

"Well, make a statement like that in a Christian youth group and someone's bound to quote a verse like Lay not up for yourself treasures upon earth'—and 50 others. So Kurt just replied in almost the exact words of Pharaoh, 'Who's the Lord anyway? I don't have to do what your Bible says.'

"Then if that wasn't enough, we heard afterwards, on very good evidence, that the guy went right back to his father and said that from what he'd found out at church, we were so keen for the land that he figured we could be squeezed for a few thousand dollars more. Talk about telling us to make bricks without straw!"

Mike couldn't resist a chuckle over the way Bill was getting worked up. The event obviously still rankled with him.

"What was so galling was the way it was having a bad effect on the group and the group's relationship with the church. I was getting blamed for leading everyone into a mess. From being enthusiastic, people were becoming not just lukewarm but really antagonistic. 'Who needs a new youth wing anyway?' they were saying. You know, I really felt for poor old Moses. I knew how he must have hurt when all his people turned on him because instead of making their lot better he'd made it worse. No wonder that by the end of chapter 5 you find him having a real bone to pick with God. I must admit I did pretty much the same thing. And just like Moses, I found God gave me just the support and encouragement I needed."

"Well, that takes you through chapter 6," joked Mike. "Are you going to go through the next six chapters plague by plague? I don't think poor old Kurt will have much chance of surviving frogs, gnats, flies, and boils!"

Bill shook his head. "No, of course that's not what happened. We got our youth wing eventually, as you know, having seen it with your own eyes. In the end Kurt did help us in the negotiations and it was as a result, I believe, of God putting pressure on his life. But it isn't the youth wing that is the crucial point as far as I'm concerned. It's Kurt himself and his relationship with the Lord. I'd willingly give up the youth wing and have the group in a tin hut if only it meant Kurt came to love and serve the Lord."

Mike saw there was a glistening in the corner of Bill's eye. A series of rapid blinks and it was gone, but in that half tear Mike realized how much Bill truly cared for Kurt. He was sorry for the jocular, half-flippant attitude he'd displayed to Bill up to now. He bit his lower lip in self-recrimination and spoke with a new seriousness.

"Tell me what happened next."

"Well, this whole controversy was producing something of a strained atmosphere in our group. At that time we would have Sunday after-church discussions in the youth den at the back of the old church. Now I have always encouraged the kids to be open and honest in their input, to pretend nothing, and to question everything they want. I've got all the time in the world for the honest doubter, having been one myself once upon a time. Usually, that has made for great times. I might not have convinced all of the kids all of the time but we've always ended up with a mutual respect."

Mike nodded in agreement. He too loved the fresh air of open debate.

"But Kurt was different. He was definitely there to spoil. There's no doubt he's a brilliant boy with a brain in the super-league class. And the stuff he's read! All those heavyweight philosophers you will only have heard of in Bible college as swearwords. Evolution and revolution and every other contentious subject—he knew something about them all. No, he knew a *lot* about them all. What was worse, he *knew* he knew a lot. And there I was with my puny Bible college diploma and a scrapbook of cuttings from *Reader's Digest*!"

Mike allowed his plain underselling of himself to pass without comment.

After a pause to taste and spit out the by now stone-cold coffee, Bill carried on. "Anyway, here we are in this group. We might be talking about Jesus being born of a virgin. Kurt would say something like 'Hey, hold on a minute. What's so great about that?' and then he would go on to produce evidence that some ancient religion or another also claimed virgin birth for a god. Or we could be discussing Jesus walking on the water, and he would tell us how some scholars suggest Jesus was really walking on a barely-submerged sandbank. And so it would go on. Everything that we said God did he would either say 'No He didn't' or 'Men can do that too.' I couldn't help being reminded . . . . "

"Don't tell me," Mike interrupted, "the way the miracles performed through Moses were duplicated by Pharaoh's magicians."

"Yep, you got it. Just look at one of those occasions. See in chapter 7, verses 8-13. Aaron's staff became a snake, and Pharaoh's magicians produced the same phenomenon. But notice how Aaron's staff swallowed up the others. In a way, that is how it was with Kurt in these discussions. He didn't always get away with it, you see. We have some pretty sharp people in the group who really know their stuff and often they would win the point over Kurt simply because they knew their Bibles and knew their Lord. But winning the point wasn't the same as winning Kurt. Just like verse 13 says about Pharaoh, his 'heart became hard and he would not listen to them.'

"It really looked as though Kurt had us all beat. He seemed to hold all the cards and he enjoyed it. He laughed at the stew we were getting into over the deal with his father. He never would admit he'd ever lost one of those discussions and he had the kind of life-style most people would envy: plenty of money from his father, good sports ability, and a high school record that mapped him out for a great career ahead. He was all set to be *the* highflyer of all time—and he'd broken a few altitude records already.

"But then things began to go wrong. At first, just little things. Like smashing up his MG."

"That's small?" Mike cried out incredulously, thinking of his own modest and elderly Bug that he'd left back home in Britain, its hood and his pride dented after a trivial entanglement with a gatepost. The incident had nearly broken his heart.

"It's small to the Neilsen family. They can buy cars like you would buy popcorn. But what bugged Kurt wasn't the write-off itself, but his Dad's refusal to cough up anything for a new one.

"Anyway, the insurance helped get him on wheels again, but then other things happened. He got dropped from the school football squad, and within a month he flunked a really important exam. He couldn't believe it; he'd never failed anything in school before. His father wasn't too happy about that either. The effect on Kurt was to make him even harder to handle in the youth group. Man, he really fouled up the discussions during that period."

"Hold on a minute." Mike lifted his hand to halt Bill's flow of words. "Are you suggesting these things were sent by God as some kind of punishment, just like the Lord sent the plagues on Pharaoh?"

"I don't think any of us can say that kind of thing dogmatically because none of us is in the heavenly senate, with God consulting us about His actions. But what I do believe on the basis of Scripture is that when we're walking contrary to God's will, He'll send warnings. That's what the prophets were about, wasn't it, telling the people to turn before it was too late? Now if God doesn't change, He must still be in the warning business. I think God was saying, 'Kurt—watch out. You can't take me on and win.'"

"Just like Pharaoh?" said Mike.

"Just like Pharaoh," Bill agreed.

"In that case, I have an even bigger problem." Mike responded.

"Something I've never been able to understand in the Bible. That is, the way that over and over again it says that it was God who hardened Pharaoh's heart, so he couldn't repent. Look, here . . . . " He pointed to the open page of his Bible at Exodus 7:3. "And here . . . . " He flipped over the pages to 9:12. "And here again . . . . " He pointed to the opposite page, his finger coming to rest at 10:1. "Then, as if that wasn't enough, Paul drives the point home in Romans 9:17 and 18."

Mike stopped, a little fearful that he had given the appearance of not believing the Bible. "What I mean is, how does it all relate to Pharaoh or to Kurt? Is God fair to them or not?"

Bill drew a pensive breath and paused a little before replying. "You'll be relieved to hear I've had problems along that line too. But the way I've worked it out is this. First of all, regarding Pharaoh. We've got to bear in mind that God had a very special purpose. He was going to demonstrate to the whole world His mighty power to save. The proof that His plan worked is that to this day the Jews still exist, and incidentally, still celebrate Passover, which was the climax to the whole Pharaoh operation. Not only that, but you and I believe in Jesus who came as the Messiah of that delivered people. None of that would have happened if God had delivered Israel with a whimper instead of a roar. That's the positive purpose we must never lose sight of. Like Paul says in his quotation of the Old Testament in Romans 9:17, 'For the Scripture says to Pharaoh: "I raised you up for this very purpose, that I might display my power in you and that my name might be proclaimed in all the earth."' Now there just wouldn't be the same effect if the first time Moses went to Pharaoh and said, 'We want to go,' the king of Egypt simply replied, 'Fine. Will tomorrow do?' The magnitude of their salvation is what has stamped Israel right up to this time. People still marvel at the stars, but no one is awed by a flashlight bulb.

"OK. I know that all I've said makes Pharaoh seem more like a fall-guy than ever, but I think there's a little clue in the way God spoke from the burning bush to Moses about the Egyptians."

Bill took the Bible from Mike's lap and thumbed his way back to Exodus 3. "See here in verse 7, 'The Lord said "I have indeed seen the misery of my people in Egypt. I have heard them crying out because of their slave drivers and I am concerned about their sufferings."' Now that says to me that Pharaoh and his henchmen already had their hearts hard as stone. How else could they so ruthlessly and cruelly have exploited the poor Israelites? So when God hardened Pharaoh's heart to resist the pleas for release, He was only doing what Pharaoh wanted anyway. *That* is surely the point: Pharaoh *wanted* a hard heart. And he got it."

Mike didn't look as though he was entirely convinced, but he felt he was a little closer to the truth. "So what you're really saying is that through God in His sovereign freedom hardened Pharaoh's heart and raised him up just so He could demonstrate His power in overthrowing him, yet Pharaoh is still 100 percent responsible for his sin?"

"That's about it," replied Bill. He noticed the traces of a frown still puckering Mike's face. He laughed, "Mike, we'll never understand it fully 'til we get to heaven. But never let go of this text: 'Will not the Judge of all the earth do right?' Genesis 18:25."

"What about Kurt?"

"Kurt went on fighting against God. The gospel was preached faithfully to him week after week in the youth group, in the church, in all kinds of ways. But you know there's an old saying, 'The same sun that melts the wax hardens the clay,' and instead of responding to God's grace and mercy, he just seemed to get more and more hostile.

"Then something really hit him. You remember I told you he'd lost his place on the football squad? Well the reason for that was that the coach saw he was beginning to fumble the ball—his coordination seemed to be slipping. Nobody put much importance on that—except Kurt himself, of course. But then he began to stumble occasionally and he complained of numbness in his legs."

"M.S.?" Mike butted in, "multiple sclerosis?"

"You've got it," said Bill. "Once it was diagnosed, Kurt went to pieces. So did his father. With no faith and all their ambitions fixed on this world and what it has to offer, it seemed like the end. They knew the pathway led from increasing debility to eventual and complete immobility. They tried every kind of cure, conventional and otherwise. Then Kurt came to me and said what must have been the costliest sentence of his life. He said, 'Bill, will you and the group pray for me?' The irony of the situation was that the very last discussion before the doctor's diagnosis was one on prayer. We had been sharing testimonies of how the Lord had answered us and Kurt blasted in with loads of guff about auto-suggestion, hypnosis, wishful thinking, and all kinds of arguments like that. He'd been at his worst. And now, here he was asking for prayer. The group was marvelous. I was really proud of them. They were already praying anyway, but after Kurt's request they intensified their petitions like I'd never have believed. Some fasted, others mounted a 24-hour prayer chain. It was great to be part of it. We had a special prayer service in the church one Sunday night. What an atmosphere!"

"And what happened?" Mike asked.

"Mike," Bill said, "it is easily the most spectacular answer to prayer I've ever experienced. Nothing immediate happened in that service that we were aware of, but over the following weeks Kurt's sensations of numbness became less frequent and he stopped falling over. I know that M.S. sufferers often have remissions of the disease when they seem to get better and then relapse. But Kurt got better all the time. The really thrilling moment was when he got his place back on the football squad."

"A storybook conversion."

Bill's face fell. "No, that's the sad part. You know, while Kurt was ill, he was really approachable. He actually talked about the Lord without a sneer in his voice. As far as the land for the youth wing was concerned, well, he and his father couldn't do enough for us. All the objections and obstructions that had been put up before melted away and we got it real cheap.

"But once Kurt was well again, all the old skepticism returned. He first began to voice doubts about whether it had been the prayer after all. 'Perhaps I would have been cured anyway,' he would say. Then he began to accuse us of manipulating him when he was vulnerable because of his illness. It was just like Pharaoh letting the Israelites go, then deciding he'd made a huge mistake and chasing after them. I think if it were possible Kurt would have tried to get his Dad to get the land back from us."

"What happened next?" Mike asked.

"Kurt left us."

"But you've still got his file on your computer," Mike observed.

Bill smiled, "Well, you're taking over, aren't you?"

Chapter 3

Mike leaned back pensively on his stool.

"You know," he said, "that's a pretty depressing start. I think I'll go back to England."

Bill grinned. "Cheer up, pal. Now for the good news!" His fingers flipped over the keyboard. "Here's someone as nice as Kurt is nasty."

Mike found himself staring at green letters spelling out the name "Pat Schwartz: Age 18. Address: 595 Easter Boulevard. Tel: 555-9721." His eye ran quickly to the paragraph of print headed "Comments" and read: "Easily overlooked. Ordinary girl from ordinary background. Easily lost in a crowd. Goes out with nice guy, Ben—also ordinary. Pat and her guy are not the 'doing' sort. Uncomplaining passengers."

Mike then looked at the bottom left corner of the screen for Bill's code letters. *Ma* he read.

"Guess?" said Bill.

"Well, I'm sure it's not Malachi," responded his friend. "Mary? But which one? Martha's sister?"

"Close—try again."

"The virgin? Jesus' mother?"

"Right on!" congratulated the older man.

"Sounds interesting," Mike commented, "but I don't see

how your comments about Pat tie up with Mary. And we don't get told much about her either, come to think of it. Seems you could be straining things to try and make Pat her counterpart. In fact, if I were Pat and knew you had done that, I think I'd be pretty scared, like I was going to have to do something pretty far out for God."

Bill swung around in his chair to face Mike.

"Ah, yes, but that's just the point. Don't you see? Mary didn't *do* anything for God; she was just her own sweet self and God did something for her. Something way, way, beyond anything she could ever have imagined. Mary is the supreme example in the Bible of what I call passive, accepting faith. That's not the only kind of faith. There is an active, aggressive faith which is just as important. In fact, both are indispensable. They belong together, two halves that make a whole, the nut and bolt that hold us together spiritually. But so often we think only of the active faith that moves mountains, parts the Red Sea, starts and stops a drought, and so on.

"The trouble is, we identify a certain type of person with that kind of faith and expect everyone to be the same. If we're honest we have to admit that even as Christians we get attracted by the glamorous and the thrilling.

"We assume that God always has His most exciting assignments for the dramatic extrovert person. If someone has been converted from a life of drugs, crime, mayhem, and murder, well, praise the Lord. And no doubt He'll use that guy or girl to bring others into the kingdom through their testimony.

"But Pat isn't that kind of girl and I don't believe Mary in the Bible was either. I think it was one of your own countrymen, Mike, a Bible teacher called Graham Scroggie who said once that it was as great a miracle for God to divert someone from sin as to deliver him from it."

"Point taken," said Mike. Fresh from Bible college, he couldn't stop a flutter of doubt from crossing his mind however. "But you're not saying Pat—or Mary for that matter—*aren't* sinners, are you?"

Bill laughed, "Getting worried about my theology? It's OK—I'm sound enough to be rung in a steeple. No, of course I'm not making Pat or Mary out to be sinless. And God sees us all on that same level of needing a blood-bought forgiveness if we're to be fit for heaven. But I'm just trying to show how we can make people feel guilty about not being guilty. We can give the impression they've got to have committed some particularly heinous crime so that they can have a Paul-sized conversion and a testimony with drama in every comma. Let me tell you a bit more about Pat, and at the same time we'll have a quick flip through what the Bible says about Mary. You'll be surprised how it all ties up."

Mike was wholly absorbed. "Carry on," he said, and he reached for his Bible where it rested on one of Bill's packing cases.

"It seems to me," began Bill, "that Mary's attitude is summed up in her words to the angel when she was first told about the amazing thing that was going to happen to her. Here it is, Luke 1:38." Bill stabbed his finger at his New Testament and Mike quickly thumbed through his Bible to the same place.

"I am the Lord's servant . . . . May it be to me as you have said," read the younger man.

"That's it. OK, now you just think about that—what kind of faith that showed. It illuminates Mary's character a whole lot. It really points up the immense quiet trust she had. I find her serenity staggering, given the mind-blowing things she'd just been told. Just think, Mike. Suppose you were a young peasant girl instead of the macho, all-male muscle-man you plainly are. And suppose you had been told that you were going to get pregnant without any human touching you, in fact, before you ever had a chance to get married to your fiancé. And that this miracle baby was going to be none other than the Son of God. How do you think you'd react?"

Mike rippled his brow in a frown and puckered his lips together. After a moment he spoke somewhat hesitantly. "Well, having three sisters, I hesitate to ever know how a woman would react. But to tell you the truth, I might not believe it had really happened. I think I might just look in the wine jar to see if someone had laced it with a hallucinogenic mushroom. If I pinched myself and found I was still seeing the angel, then I would have to take it seriously. After that, well, I guess I'd zip around to Joseph's house and say, 'Hey, guess what!'"

Bill grinned broadly. "Maybe it's a good thing you're not a girl and that you're not living at the time Christ was due to come, for that sure isn't the response God was looking for from Mary. I'm sure He'd been observing her for a long time, because the Bible says she found favor with God and He knew He could trust her to believe and keep His secret. I'm sure that she didn't even tell Joseph, because when you read Matthew's account of Jesus' birth, you find that the poor man didn't have a clue what was happening until he himself had a divine revelation in a dream. Up to then he thought he was going to have to discreetly part from his pregnant girlfriend.

"Anyway," continued Bill, "Mary showed this immense capacity for simply receiving on trust what she was told—even welcoming it, though it would be the revolution of her life. As I said, this is passive faith at its best."

"Granted," Mike interjected, "but how does this link up with Pat from the youth group?"

"Well, she hasn't been given any mighty revelation and obviously she certainly isn't giving birth to the Messiah. But I believe that the same sensitive, obedient faith that Mary had flows out from Pat. And just a couple of months ago she proved how real that faith is."

Mike sensed from Bill's changed tone of voice that a new seriousness had come into the conversation.

Bill waved his hand at the monitor. "There's something missing from that screen. I haven't updated the file. I haven't had the heart to."

Mike noticed that the natural laughter lines on Bill's face had changed into a frown of sadness.

"In fact, I can hardly talk about what happened without choking over the whole thing even now. It will be eight weeks ago next Saturday. We were all down at the church just doing our normal recreation night thing. Pat was there waiting for her fiancé, Ben, to arrive. A load of us were playing volleyball. I was right beside her and we were having a real great time, laughing and messing up the game. I was trying to get her out of her shy-

underestimate the folk who exhibit passive faith. A crisis really shows what we're made of."

"What's her secret?" asked Mike.

"Secret? A pretty open one—she abides in the Lord. So when her world blew to bits, she had spiritual reserves which kept her going with hardly a falter."

Bill grew thoughtful. "You know, I see another parallel with Mary. Do you recall how, after Jesus was born and the shepherds had come to see Him, Luke tells us that 'Mary treasured up all these things and pondered them in her heart'? Uh—you'll find that in Luke 2:19," he added, as he saw Mike having some difficulty blowing on the page edges of his Bible to separate them. Then as Mike succeeded at last, Bill went on, "And just look at the next column. See, in verse 35, there's Mary bringing Jesus to the Temple in a kind of dedication service, and hearing all sorts of wonderful things about her new baby son. And then this old guy Simeon said something that must have made her stomach feel like she was going down a roller coaster with the end of the track missing. He said, 'A sword will pierce your own soul too.' Now, how does a mother face bringing up a son with that hanging over her? Just when every new mother has all kinds of exciting dreams about her infant's future, she is told she is going to have sorrow and pain.

"I bet that memory echoed a lot down the years, especially when she eventually stood under that cross.

"But I think I do know how she lived with that disturbing prophecy of Simeon's. And that was by constant communing with God. She was at perfect rest in Him, so whether she was thinking of the shepherd's happy talk or Simeon's solemn warning, she was at peace."

"Don't you think she ever got worried?" queried Mike.

"She must have. After all, she was very, very human. At one time she even went with her other sons to rescue Jesus from the crowd because they thought He might be going mad."

Mike raised a quizzical eyebrow. "You sure? I remember Jesus' brothers doing something like that, but surely not His mother, too?"

"It's right there in Mark's Gospel." Bill pushed across his

open Bible without waiting for Mike to unstick more reluctant pages.

"See, here in chapter 3, verse 21 tells us His family went to take charge of Him because, they said, 'He is out of his mind.' Now just a little further on in verse 31 it tells us right out who was in that family deputation: 'Jesus' mother and brothers.'"

"So Mary didn't have perfect understanding?"

"No, she was prone to worry like any mother would. I mean, she sure had a lot to take on board in her motherhood. Like a son who disappears for three days when He's 12 years old and then turns up in the Temple among the professors like He was one of them—only more so. Then there was the time at the wedding in Cana in John 2. It must have been a bit hard to have Jesus say to her, 'Why do you involve me?' when she asked Him to help the family out of their no-wine crisis. Jesus knew what He was doing, of course. But the wonderful thing is, so did Mary. So she simply tells the servants to get on with it and do whatever Jesus says. It all goes to show that this close contact with God I've talked about was able to carry her through every thing; the anxieties, the puzzles, the apparent rebuffs, right up to the cross itself when that sword pierced her own soul."

"And you reckon that's where Pat gets her strength, too?"

"Sure do. I'm certain of it. I know she prays a lot and though, like Mary, she might have a down period, she comes on through."

Bill reached out to the computer keyboard again, ready to key up the next file.

"I'll leave you to alter that information when you take the printout with you. What do you think you'll put?"

Mike did not answer immediately. Then he said, "Well, I'll put in the bare outline of her losing Ben. And then I'll delete the bit about 'Uncomplaining passenger.' Wait a minute, though. I don't think I will. That's just what she is; that's her secret—a passenger carried along by the grace of God, totally trusting Him to bring her through." Mike paused. "And I guess I want to be on board, too."

Chapter 4

Mike stretched his arms above his head to relieve muscles cramped by prolonged hunching on the uncomfortable stool. "One loser, one winner," he said. "That makes it a tie so far. We greet our viewers to this exciting ball game wondering which way this breathtaking contest will go now."

Bill grinned and opened his mouth to reply but was interrupted by the brash *brrring* of the telephone.

Burrowing under a pile of papers by the side of the computer, sending squadrons of them into disorganized flight, he fished out the receiver and nestled it under his chin while he tried to retrieve the airborne sheets.

"Bill Pulkington. Hi." His craggy face split into a large smile and the laughter lines danced. Obviously, someone he's glad to hear from, thought Mike.

Short, happy phrases spilled out from Bill's lips and Mike guessed the half of the conversation at the other end of the line was just as warm. Eventually, with a final "Great. See you tomorrow," Bill released the phone from his chin and reburied it in the pile of papers on its hidden rest.

His face still beaming like California sunshine, he turned to Mike. "Well, that's just the neatest coincidence. I was just about to answer your question as to who's next on my file, and the man himself buzzes me."

"Do I get a prize if I guess right that we've got a winner?" Mike queried.

Bill's smile widened still further to the point where it threatened to wrap around his ears. "Uh-huh. But only if I can have a prize for prophesying the sun will rise tomorrow. That was my right-hand man in the youth group, Joe Miller. He's been my lieutenant for a couple of years now. What an asset."

"Then if there are no prizes for guessing he's a winner, can I have one for guessing you're going to match him up with Timothy?"

"Maybe I'll give you an extra cup of coffee. Anyway, let's call him up."

Bill settled himself in front of his pride and joy and began once more to flash his practiced fingers over the keyboard.

Like the genie in the lamp, the screen obeyed its master's wishes and spread the familiar format. This time Mike glanced at the bottom left-hand corner first and noticed to his satisfaction the code letters *Ti* indicating his guess had been right. He observed Joe's age, 21, and then read silently to himself the comments. "Was LEPSOG. Now real faith. Shy, diffident, lacks confidence. Loyal, gentle, feels deeply. Physically weak. Leadership potential, but doesn't believe it."

"LEPSOG? Your computer's lost a tooth from its byte."

"Nope—that's what I put in and that's what's meant to be there. It's my own word. It won't get into Webster's until the next edition."

"OK, let me in. What's it mean?"

"It's someone who knows the gospel backwards. G-O-S-P-E-L, L-E-P-S-O-G. Get it?"

Mike was plainly unimpressed.

"You see," Bill went on, "I've found over the years that some of the most difficult kids to get through to are those who have been familiar with Christian things all their lives. When they've had good-living parents, been brought up in Sunday School and church, they can have so much of the Christian fragrance clinging to their clothes they can fool you—even themselves—that they've got the genuine essence of it too. That's especially true if they are the sort that, by temperament, tend to be compliant, never stepping out of line; you know, the sort that always collects Sunday School merit awards like dogs collect fleas—unwanted but unstoppable."

"I know what you mean," said Mike. "I was a bit like that when I was little. I hated it. I would try deliberately not to win just so I wouldn't be made to look different from my friends. I *seemed* good to my teachers, but I knew inside I was just as much a sinner as anyone else, with all sorts of wrong desires and thoughts. It was just that I lacked the courage to carry those desires out."

"Right," replied Bill. "In fact, I think lack of courage is often a component part of that particular temperament. It's something I've noticed in Joe, and it's certainly something the Bible shows to be true in Timothy."

"So that makes three of us," Mike said warmly, glad to know that he wasn't alone in his self-doubt and lack of confidence. The thought of the job ahead of him, taking over this youth group from the experienced and successful Bill filled him with apprehension.

Bill halted Mike's train of thought for the moment, however, and brought back his newly-invented LEPSOG.

"I know it isn't quite the same with Timothy as with my friend Joe, because the gospel itself was fairly new to everybody. But there's just a hint that Timothy had a bit of a barrier to be broken down. It's that little glimpse we get of his home life in the second letter Paul wrote him."

Bill paused while Mike turned his Bible pages. He continued, "Look in the first chapter at verse 5. Paul talks of Timothy's faith as first living in his grandmother Lois and in his mother Eunice and now living in him also. Then later on in the fifteenth verse of chapter 3, he comments that Timothy has known the Scriptures from infancy."

Mike interrupted, "I don't quite see how that fits in with what Acts 16 says about Timothy meeting Paul. There he seems to have been converted along with his mother."

This time it was Bill who was flicking through his Bible. "Let's see . . . yes, I've got it. Paul 'came to Derbe and then to Lystra, where a disciple named Timothy lived, whose mother was a Jewess and a believer, but whose father was a Greek,'" Bill read. He looked up and asked, "What's the problem?"

"Well, it seems that Timothy was a believer from the first time Paul came to Lystra in chapter 14."

"Granted, but that doesn't mean that his mother and grandmother couldn't have been converted first. In fact, it may be that Timothy was converted through their witness in between the Apostle's two visits in Lystra, though I doubt that since Paul so often calls Timothy his son, which he would probably only do if he were converted directly under his ministry. Anyway, whatever our guesses, I stick to my main point. Paul rejoiced over a living faith that Timothy now possessed a faith that wasn't there before. And that's just how it was with Joe. I had assumed when I came he was already a Christian (he was only 11 then). His life seemed so consistent.

"But I'll never forget the day he came to me five years later and said, 'Bill, I'm not sure whether I'm a Christian or not.' So I said, 'Well why not go home, kneel by your bed and tell the Lord that, and then say, "Lord, whether I am yours already or not, I now unreservedly give myself to you in repentance and faith. Come into my life, Lord Jesus."' He went away and did just that."

"Did you see a big difference in him?"

"In one way, yes; in another way, no. The difference showed itself to me in that when he talked of the Lord it was much more real. Before, it was a kind of secondhand thing, but now you could tell he was talking from personal experience. But I'm sure a lot of people who weren't tuned in didn't notice anything. He was still to them just Mr. Nice Guy, whom they'd known all their lives and assumed to be a Christian."

"You know, I think we can make a big mistake when we talk of people being changed by the Lord. Of course, He does change lots of the things, the most important being our move from death to life. But there are some things that don't change. Your personality and temperament are still what they were before you accepted Christ. Once a jerk, always a jerk!" grinned Mike.

"Maybe," said Bill, "but what we do get is power to overcome the weaknesses and straighten out the kinks, plus some well-directed pummeling from the Lord to knock out the dents, and a few snips from the pruning shears to cut off the dead wood."

Mike thoughtfully flicked the pages of his Bible under his thumb until he came to Acts 16. "I think you're right," he said. "We're told here that Paul picked Timothy to go with him on his missionary journey. So he must have been very impressed with the youngster as a potential fellow worker. He must have made huge strides in a short time for the Apostle to want to take him on board. And yet in other parts of the New Testament we find out that Timothy was liable to fear and that he lacked the personal charisma to have any natural authority over people. I'm thinking of that time when Paul wanted to send Timothy to Corinth."

Mike once again ran the Bible under his thumb. He rapidly scanned Paul's first Corinthian letter looking for a half-remembered verse. "Yes, here it is—chapter 16, verses 10 and 11: 'If Timothy comes, see to it that he has nothing to fear while he is with you, for he is carrying on the work of the Lord, just as I am. No one, then, should refuse to accept him. Send him on his way in peace so that he may return to me.' Do you get the impression, Bill, that Paul is trying to cover for him, afraid that Timothy might get as much notice as a cricket in a field?"

"Right," Bill assented. "And when you read Second Corinthians, it looks as though Paul's fears were justified."

"How come?" puzzled the Englishman. "We don't read anything about him there that I can remember."

"That's just the point. For although he's with Paul then, as the opening greeting shows, the messenger Paul talks about is Titus, as you'll see in 2 Corinthians 7:6 and 12:18. The obvious conclusion is that Timothy's mission had been a flop."

"But it wasn't always like that, was it?"

"Good grief, no! That's the thing I find so heartening. Timothy was far from perfect, yet God could use him. Just think about what we know of him: he was shy to the point of fearfulness so that Paul had to rebuke him for his spirit of fear and warn him about being ashamed of the Lord (2 Tim. 1:8); he was unimpressive, as the non-event of his visit to Corinth showed; he was far enough from perfect holiness to have to be warned by Paul about 'the evil desires of youth' (2 Tim. 2:22); and then, just to make things more difficult, he tended to get sick a lot (1 Tim. 5:23). Add to that the fact that he was young anyway, and you have a near-certain failure application for the job of Apostle's Assistant. Yet Paul took him on. And that's even more remarkable when you remember he'd only just fired Mark for letting him down. Seems on the surface Paul was inviting trouble."

Mike was thinking hard about himself. All his inadequacies, his fear of failure, and the constant burning wish he had that God had made him differently swirled around his mind. But that very insecurity made him unwilling to expose his own soul to the man he was taking over for, so he phrased his question around the two young men they had been talking about.

"Why do you think Paul chose Timothy? And why did you pick Joe?"

Bill chuckled. Years of experience had made him a difficult man to fool. "You mean why did I choose *you*! Well, the answer for all three of you is the same—it's God's call. The Bible tells us that the Lord doesn't take the self-sufficient, but rather, the 'weak and foolish' as it calls them."

"That's me alright," muttered Mike.

"Well, cheer up. The gospel is good news for nobodies. That's you—and me. And now you'll want to ask, 'What are the marks of a call to service?' Let's think about Timothy first. Paul tells him not to give in to his natural fear, not because he has any resources of his own, but because God has given him the gift of the Holy Spirit (2 Tim. 1:6,7). Then again, Paul reminds him that God has given him a special gift for the job and that respected leaders of the church were there at the time to recognize his calling (1 Tim. 4:14). He didn't have to be at the mercy of his wavering subjective feelings, his soul bobbing up and down like an empty soda can on the ocean, threatening to be swamped at any moment.

"And that's how it was with Joe. When he was about 17 or 18 I began to notice a quality in his handling of affairs in the group that said something to me. It was the way he talked to others and the thoroughness of every job he did. He's never been a great speaker or counselor or anything. But everything he's done he's done well, and always with a quiet reliance on the Lord. If he had rushed up to me and said, 'I've been called to be your assistant leader' I'd have written him off as a fraud. But he really proved himself in all kinds of small ways. And that's just like Timothy. The really significant sentence in the beginning of his story there in Acts 16 is where we're told, 'The brothers at Lystra and Iconium spoke well of him' (v. 2). Let me tell you what really impressed me about Joe. It was when we were having that crisis over Kurt and the ground for the new youth wing. There was all this hassle going on like I told you, with everything, just everything collapsing around my ears. All kinds of bickering and squabbling and those discussion nights with Kurt sometimes mopping the floor with me—it's the nearest I've ever gotten to chucking the whole thing in. Well, during that time Joe would come around here, sometimes two or three times a week. I can see him now just pushing his head so shyly around that door and saying, 'Can I come in a minute?' He'd come with some small point or another apparently to get help but I knew all along it was because he wanted to help and encourage me. He wouldn't stay long, but he'd always end up with prayer, thanking me for my help. It was great. I think that's when I really knew he was a true Timothy, because that's exactly what you find Paul so thrilled about. It's loyalty—pure, godly loyalty. You know, there can't be many more moving passages in the New Testament than 2 Timothy 4:9 in the end. It's probably the last thing in the Bible we have from Paul's pen. Paul thinks his death can't be far away. And the tragedy is, he's almost entirely alone. One of his former fellow workers, Demas, has turned away and deserted him and only Luke is left. So Paul appeals to Timothy, 'Do your best to come to me quickly' (v. 9) and then right at the end he repeats the plea, 'Do your best to get here before winter' (v. 21). That's how much Paul thought of his son in the faith."

Mike felt cheered by Bill's words. He also looked forward to having Joe, whom he had not yet met, working alongside him. It was great to think of God using people in spite of their problems. In fact, he thought, maybe God could only use those who knew they were weak, or else they would rely on themselves instead of Him.

Mike said, "I did a special study on Timothy in my last semester at Bible college, but the passage you quoted never quite struck me like that before. It certainly ties in with all those assignments Paul gave Timothy: Thessalonica, Corinth, Berea, Macedonia, Ephesus, Philippi. Unless Paul was sure of a huge degree of loyalty he could never have trusted him with all that."

"Yes, you're absolutely right. And because of that, the apparent failure at Corinth didn't matter all that much. Timothy had done his best with the gifts God had given him. The responsibility wasn't his if the Corinthians didn't listen to him. Paul never held success over him. He simply told him not to be afraid and to stir up the gift God had given him. Of course, if Timothy had stayed moping around at his failures and neglected God's gift, that would have been different. I'm sure Paul would have had some stormy words for him then."

"What other qualities do Timothy and your Joe share?" Mike asked.

"I'm glad you asked me that," Bill replied, "because I don't think I've mentioned the most important thing that I've valued Joe for, though I've hinted at it. And that is his level of sheer *caring*. In this regard, I really do feel like Paul felt about Timothy. You mentioned just now the assignment Paul gave to Timothy to visit Philippi. Do you recall the glowing tribute the Apostle gave him?"

"Not off hand" Mike admitted.

"Look it up in your Bible; it's really worth reading in full. You'll find it in Philippians 2:19 and the next couple of verses."

Mike obediently found the place and began to read. "I hope in the Lord Jesus to send Timothy to you soon, that I also may be cheered when I receive news about you. I have no one else like him, who takes a genuine interest in your welfare. For everyone looks out for his own interests, not those of Jesus Christ. But you know that Timothy has proved himself, because as a son with his father he has served with me in the work of the gospel."

Mike looked up from the ancient letter. "That's terrific.

Fancy having the greatest Christian who ever lived saying about you—'I have no one else like him.'" Mike looked wistful. "I don't suppose anyone would ever feel that about me."

Bill roared with laughter. "Mike, that's not what it's all about. We're not here to get human accolades. As long as the Lord approves, that's all that matters. No, it seems to me the very essence of Timothy was that he *wasn't* bothered about what people thought of him, though his natural inclination and temperament must have pointed him that way. Everyone else looked out for his own interests but Timothy simply *cared* for others. I think that word 'genuine' in verse 20 is quite significant too. When we're given responsibility to run the youth group or any other part of the Lord's work, we know we *ought* to care, but we don't, so we pretend. That wasn't Timothy! Paul tells us of Timothy's tears at one point (2 Tim. 1:4). That's the mark of the man's caring concern."

"How do we get there? How can we be like Timothy?" There was a passionate edge to Mike's words which did not go unnoticed by Bill.

The youth pastor responded with as reassuring a tone of voice as he could. "Mike, if you can ask that question in the way you've just asked it, you're already on the way and I want you to know I've got every confidence you're going to make it. Prophecy is not a gift the Lord has given me in abundance, but I'm going to make one. Give yourself a year here at Fairmont and I'll guarantee by then you'll have been on the verge of resigning 52 times. But the Lord will have stopped you 53. You'll find that those kids will have so tunneled into your heart you won't be able to drive them out. They'll cause you a lot of pain there, but you'll prefer the pain to the echoing emptiness of a heart with no one to care for. Most of all, you'll find like Paul did, 'Christ's love compels us' (2 Cor. 5:14). In other words, Mike, you don't have to worry about making yourself care as though it were some kind of academic or athletic goal. As long as you're true to the Lord and willing to be vulnerable, it will just happen. On the other hand, if you put up the shutters and don't let people get through to you, you'll have an easier time, but you'll miss God's best. Paul had to remind Timothy to endure hardship like a good soldier of Jesus Christ; he could not afford to let himself get deflected from his task anymore than a soldier could get tangled up in civilian affairs when he was supposed to be on duty (2 Tim. 2:3,4)."

Mike realized what a challenge was facing him, taking over from this man who was so obviously speaking from experience when he talked of the suffering of caring. Any ideas of glamour connected with the job of youth pastor at Fairmont, and any feelings of being flattered at getting the position, melted. Yet those laughter lines that were forever wrinkling into smiles on Bill's face told him there was joy in the job too.

Bill's grin was spreading across his face right then. "OK, I think we've said enough about you and Timothy for now. We've almost forgotten the one who started this whole conversation—Joe. Tell you what. You come and meet him tomorrow. You'll be two Timothys together. You'll get along well."

"That'll be great," responded Mike enthusiastically.

"Right. Now before our next file, how about another cup of coffee? But I warn you—you'll need it strong. We've got two coming up who are pretty hard to take."

Chapter 5

Mike stared at the quarter-inch of thick goo lying in the bottom of his mug. When Bill talked about making it strong, he meant it. Still, it was hot and sweet and Mike felt refreshed and relaxed.

"I'm ready. What—or who's—next?"

"Like I said, I've got two people I want us to look at. Actually, they're husband and wife—or I should say, they were. They're both dead now, killed in a car crash a few years ago. I was only involved with them a short time when I first came, but they'd been around for quite a while before then. In fact, they were in leadership."

He paused, then added, "Don't ask me how that was. They certainly weren't fit to be leaders. In fact, I'm certain the wife wasn't a Christian at all. Funny things can happen in churches, though Fairmont wasn't as strong then as it is now and I guess people were desperate for help and took whoever they could get. And, boy, was she a forceful character. She just took over."

"Hold on a minute," interjected Mike. "If all you say is true, and if they are both dead, why have you still got them on file?"

"Because they are such a lesson and a warning to us all. Apart from which," he continued with an impish grin, "I'm pretty pleased with myself for the Bible parallel I made right there in the early days. It proved to be right on."

Mike put his mug on the floor and picked up his Bible. "I'm all ears, Bill. Lead on."

"OK, let's get them up on the screen first." Bill's deft manipulations produced the desired effect and they both stared at the resulting image, reading silently.

"Abe and Cindy Chalk: youth leaders, deceased.

"Abe: weak-willed, immature, selfish.

"Cindy: strong, domineering, worldly.

"*AJ.*"

"Wow!" exclaimed Mike. "You don't believe in never speaking ill of the dead, do you?"

"Well, Mike, as you know this *is* a confidential file. You're the only person to have seen it apart from Joe and myself. And there's no point in putting fibs up there. I use it as a reminder and a warning, and a spur to my praying. It helps me to watch out for others who might be beginning to show the same traits so I can step in early to try and bring some loving and firm counsel before it's too late. Those two might have been losers, but if their story can help someone else to get on the winning side, then they've served some purpose."

"Alright, I agree. But I see your Bible code is *AJ*. Now that can only mean Ahab and Jezebel. That's coming on a bit strong, isn't it? I mean, as far as I can remember, they're just about the most evil characters in the whole Bible."

As with the discussion on Kurt, Mike, who had the commendable tendency to always see the best in everyone, seemed set to defend the mysterious Abe and Cindy.

Bill, with the patience born of years of talking with young people, leaned back in his chair to reply. "Of course I can't claim that Abe and Cindy were really Ahab and Jezebel reincarnated. All I meant when I made the identification was that the same traits and characteristics were there. For example, they never murdered anyone, and those two in the Bible had Naboth killed, but the totally self-centered determination that led up to that killing was there. And they did something pretty close to it in the end."

"Alright, I'll take your word for it." He suddenly chuckled,

"Guess I'm just a proud Brit who can't give in to a Colonialist. But you've been right every time so far, so carry on."

With the atmosphere somewhat eased, Bill put his fingers tip to tip against his pursed lips as he tried to recall events of a decade ago. He began, "I was the first youth pastor Fairmont ever had. They'd always been too small to afford one before then." He grinned broadly. "I guess I came cut-price.

"Anyway, when I arrived I met Abe and Cindy, then in their early 20s. They had been married a couple of years and leading the group for about as long. Of course, the church board expected them to step down to give me a free hand, and it looked like that's what they did. However, it soon became clear that in their hearts they still regarded themselves in control. I'd made things worse for myself by saying when I first met them that *of course* I wanted them to carry on in an active role and how valuable their experience would be to a rookie like me, and how I'd really appreciate it if they kept up a high-level involvement, and so on and so forth.

"Mike, when you move to a new church, never make rash statements like that before you've had an opportunity to get to know people and pray about them. I certainly paid for my indiscretion. I found that for the first year I was continually being blocked in virtually everything I did. I felt raw and unsure of myself and I didn't want to create a fuss. Nevertheless, I had to toughen up in the end; otherwise I'd have been dishonoring the Lord and abdicating my responsibility. Now I'm a real ogre who eats youth leaders for breakfast."

"I don't believe it," said Mike.

"Well, not too often. And you're the wrong flavor! Anyway, back to Abe and Cindy. My innocence about them was shattered and my worries began within about a week. They asked me over for dinner. My, what an eye-opener! The first thing I saw when I got in their house was a porno magazine on their coffee table. I didn't take too much notice; I thought maybe they'd taken it from one of the kids in the group. I know now that would be highly unlikely.

"Well, we started to eat and they were pleasant enough at first. Then I tried, as I usually do, to steer the conversation around to get them to share their experience of the Lord with me. I told them a little bit about myself and how I came to know Christ and then I gave them the opportunity to do the same. I asked Abe first of all when he came to know the Lord. He gave some kind of muddy, incoherent testimony which, to me at least, lacked any real conviction. But I was still green enough to give everybody the benefit of the doubt, and anyway, I don't make it a habit to judge people's testimonies. Relationships with the Lord are personal affairs and we all stand before Him alone. So I let all the questionable points pass. But it was when I asked Cindy how she came to know the Lord that I got the real jolt. 'I never have,' she said, 'and I don't suppose I ever will.'"

"At least she was honest," Mike interjected. "Surely that's better than trying to pretend a faith she didn't have?"

"Granted," Bill went on, "but remember—this lady had been appointed a youth leader along with her husband. What made it worse is that when I queried her position, she could see nothing incongruous in it. As far as she was concerned, she was doing the church a favor and everyone at Fairmont ought to be mighty glad that she'd come along at the right moment and helped them out. *She* wasn't going to give up now. It was then that I began to sense she was power-hungry, and the church happened to be the unfortunate object of her indulgence."

Mike butted in again. "Coming back to my quibble about linking Abe and Cindy with Ahab and Jezebel, I can't really say I see it that close yet from what you've told me."

"Get your Bible open and I'll show you how things developed right in line with what we read in 1 Kings."

Mike opened his Bible to the appropriate place.

"Turn to chapter 16," Bill instructed. "Now look at verse 31, which kind of introduces us to Ahab. See what it says there?"

Mike read aloud: "'He not only considered it trivial to commit the sins of Jeroboam son of Nebat, but he also married Jezebel daughter of Ethbaal king of the Sidonians, and began to serve Baal and worship him.'"

"As our conversation went on," Bill said, "I realized a few things. The first was that, however real Abe's conversion might have been, it hadn't affected his values or his life-style. He spoke quite openly about cheating the tax man, for example, and even offered me advice as to how I could do it. Like Ahab, he considered such things 'trivial.' The second thing was that he had gotten himself into an unequal yoke by marrying a rank unbeliever, Cindy, just as Ahab had gotten himself into an unholy match with the pagan queen Jezebel."

"Don't you think that's overstressed?" Mike asked. "I mean, I know Paul says, 'Do not be yoked together with unbelievers' in 2 Corinthians 6:14, but so many young people have said to me, 'But we're really in love, and I'm sure God wants it. I have faith my partner will be converted in time.' Don't they have a point?"

"Sometimes that does happen. But in my 10 years here, over and over again I've seen it work the other way. We mustn't let God's sovereign grace in bringing one or two to himself via an unequally yoked marriage blind us to the plain teaching of the Word of God. Anyway, 2 Corinthians 6:14 isn't the only verse on the subject, you know. It's a pretty consistent teaching. And I think the two cases we're talking about add weight to the point. Both for Ahab and Abe Chalk, marrying an unbeliever was absolutely disastrous."

"Do their personalities have anything to do with it?" asked Mike.

"To a certain extent, yes," Bill admitted. "In fact I think this would be a good time to leave Abe and Cindy for a few minutes and try and build up a character sketch of Ahab and Jezebel. From what you read of him, Mike, what do you make of Ahab?"

Mike thought for a moment and then said, "If I had to settle on one word to describe him, I would choose 'immature.' I'm thinking especially of that incident in 1 Kings 21 when he took a fancy to Naboth's vineyard next door to his palace and wanted it for a backyard. He got so furious when Naboth said no. I seem to remember the Bible says he went home 'sullen and angry.'"

"Right," said Bill. "And that's not the only time those words are used of him. In the previous chapter he manifests the same attitude over a rebuke a prophet gives him."

"Yes, and there's that time in chapter 22 when he was going to fight alongside King Jehoshaphat who wanted some guidance from the Lord first. And all the 'yes men' prophets came and said how successful he would be. But Jehoshaphat wasn't satisfied. He must have felt it didn't ring true. So Ahab said he had one more prophet, Micaiah. But he wasn't keen to hear him because, he said, he only prophesied bad things—never anything good. That's immaturity if you like, not willing to hear the truth if it hurts."

Bill spoke encouragingly, "You've certainly hit the nail on the head. Ahab was definitely an immature, childish, weak man. And one of the chief characteristics of immaturity is a tremendous selfishness. It's 'me first' all the time, just like the baby in a crib crying for a bottle. But what's natural and endearing in a baby is grotesque in a grown man.

"Now for Jezebel. How do you see her?"

Again, Mike did not reply immediately, but took his time as he recalled the biblical incidents. "Well," he said at last, "if you want one word to describe her, I'd have to say *vixen*."

Bill chortled at the unexpected hostility so out of character in the mild-mannered Englishman. "That, young man, is very unfair to foxes, and considering that dogs were allowed to make a meal of her when she met her doom, pushed off the tower at Jezreel, I think our canine friends must be reckoned superior." He grew much more serious. "All the same, I know what you mean.

"I think the tragedy is that you have in Jezebel a tremendous potential for good which is wholly twisted towards evil. She had such strength of character she could really have been the making of her husband. Instead, she was his utter downfall and ruin. She had Ahab twisted around her little finger, and she led him from bad, to worse, to disaster. She was so domineering. Mind you, I can't help admiring the way she faced her death sentence. She knew what was going to happen and yet she had the courage to paint herself up and face Jehu without a quiver" (2 Kings 9:30-37).

"I agree," Mike said. "I've often thought of her confrontation with Elijah at the end of the drought—you know, that famous contest between the prophets of Baal and Elijah on Mount Carmel in 1 Kings 18. The Lord gave Elijah an enormous victory and the lone prophet had the 450 prophets slaughtered. He was really on top. Yet when Jezebel sent a threatening message to him, he ran away for his life. What a powerful personality that woman must have had. I mean, fancy scaring Elijah, of all people. I certainly wouldn't like to take him on."

Bill nodded, then said, "Everybody who ever lived as a potential for God—the real possibility of being one of His winners. That's what makes it so tragic when they end up as losers.

"So let's sum up the characteristics of these two and put them together to see what we've got. There's Ahab—selfish, childish, always wanting his own way and pouting if he doesn't get it. He has a nominal faith in the Lord, but only so far as it suits him. I think his battles with Ben-Hadad in 1 Kings 20 prove that. There it really looked as if Ahab had it all together, trusting the Lord and seeing victory after victory, really looking quite brave. But then when he seems to have it all sewn up, he puts his own interests first again by letting Ben-Hadad off the hook, and wham, he's in trouble again!

"On the other hand, there's Jezebel, as strong as he is weak. In fact, I get the impression she despises him. Utterly ruthless, domineering, openly hostile to Israel's faith and unashamed of pushing her own beliefs. Now, put those two together and what have you got?"

"Calamity for everybody, I would think," Mike replied. "The whole country suffers, but nobody more than the best of the people, like Elijah. In the end, Ahab and Jezebel themselves suffer. Their gross materialism, unfaithfulness, and me-first-ism is their own ruin."

Before Bill could reply, Mike added, "When you come to think of it, those are very modern problems."

"Too true," said Bill. "And I've never seen them more clearly on display than in Abe and Cindy. As that first evening with them wore on I began to feel more and more sick at heart. I found that, like Ahab, Abe trusted the Lord for as long as it suited him. For example, he was quite happy in one breath to tell me the Lord had answered his prayers when he'd had a financial problem and then in the next to say he'd blown the cash on a wild party—a party, incidentally, that Cindy had wanted.

"As for Cindy, she appalled me by telling me how a couple of weeks earlier she'd been to have her horoscope cast."

"Didn't you tell her it was wrong in God's eyes?" Mike queried incredulously.

"Sure I did—and I pulled out my pocket Bible to show her the Scriptures. But she just laughed it off and told me not to be such a jerk. Phew! I knew I had a problem on my hands.

"I went home that night and prayed like mad. Here I was, the new kid on the block, and I had these two characters as established leaders in the group. I knew I had to act, but how?

"It was way into the early hours of the morning that I decided the first thing I had to do was to go and see the pastor of the church and talk to him about it. Any action would have to have his support. So I went to see him. And I had a huge shock. He was a pleasant enough guy; I'd met him before, of course, and had good fellowship with him. He wasn't far from retiring and he was really kind and, well, nice.

"But after I'd said my piece and told him I felt Abe and Cindy had to go, that they weren't fit to be leaders, he hemmed, and hawed, he waffled around like a hen looking for corn, and then he told me, 'Bill, I agree with everything you say and I've known something about these two for a while, but I can't do anything—and you mustn't either.'

"Naturally, I was amazed and asked him why. It turned out they had a hold on that church that stemmed way back through Abe's family. You see, Abe's family had been founding members. To put it in a nutshell, what Pastor was saying was that he dare not cause an upset now which would split the church, especially at this late stage in his ministry. I'll swear he had tears in his eyes as he pleaded with me to play it cool and not rock the boat. He said he'd protected the youth group as best he could from Cindy's strange beliefs and had tried to make sure that good, sound, speakers were brought in to take their Scripture classes."

"A bit like Obadiah looking after the prophets of the Lord in the Ahab-Jezebel story," Mike interrupted.

"Yes, I thought that. But maybe like Obadiah, something stronger should have been done long before.

"Anyway, since I was new, and given the pastor's fear and the fact that I was under his authority, I decided to comply, at least for the time being. And, of course, I prayed. Boy, how I prayed.

"Well, I managed to work with them after a fashion, but I knew they didn't like me and they made life fairly uncomfortable with all sorts of minor irritations, like arranging events and not telling me. Sometimes, for instance, they would take the group out on a trip to the movies. I wouldn't have minded so much if it weren't for the fact that the movie would often turn out to be not so wholesome.

"Needless to say, with all this pulling in different directions, the group was getting nowhere. The things I was teaching about wholehearted commitment were being subtly undermined by the loose life-style of these two leaders who were supposed to be my right-hand people. The kids didn't know whether they were coming or going. I began to understand the bafflement of the Israelites on Mount Carmel as they tried to sort out whether Elijah or Jezebel was right. No wonder Elijah had to soak that sacrifice before the fire fell. It was going to need a mighty impressive miracle to get the Israelites out of their confusion."

"Did you get a miracle?" asked Mike.

"The way it worked out was weird," Bill replied. "I don't like to think God was responsible for the bad things, but I've no doubt He worked things out for His glory. This is how it happened.

"One of the characteristics of the couple was their greed. Abe, in his childish way, wanted everything. But he didn't always have the drive to get it. So Cindy, who couldn't stand his weakness, made sure he got what he wanted, no matter how.

"Well, they began to take an interest in boats and decided they wanted to own this fantastic 32-foot yacht. They didn't have the money, of course, so they decided to go into partnership with their next-door neighbors, get a five-year bank loan to cover their half, and share the boat's use.

"At first it worked OK, but after a few months they began to get fed up. Every time they wanted to take the boat out it seemed it was their neighbor's turn, and being the kind of people they were, they believed they had a right to it anytime they chose.

"There were arguments and quarrels and, in the end, the Chalks decided they would buy out their neighbors' share. They could only offer a fraction of what it was worth and naturally their neighbors laughed in their faces. Instead, they offered to buy Abe and Cindy out at the full price. Boy, did that rile them. To be balked in their own bid and then to have the counter-bid made to them was so humiliating they hardly talked to anyone for days. Abe would just have let it lie there but we could all see that Cindy was plotting all kinds of mad schemes behind that furious look she wore. But, nevertheless, we all thought it would blow over and she would simmer down. I must confess I was taking a little bit of unsanctified delight in her discomfiture at the time.

"Then things began to happen to their neighbors. Little things, like finding their locks glued up or a fire in their mailbox. Childish things—the pranks that youngsters have pulled for years. In fact, everyone assumed it was kids. The neighbors told the police, and just tried to grin and bear it. We now know differently.

"Well, the climax came one weekend when the neighbors took the boat out. It just sank for no apparent reason. They were rescued and the boat was salvaged. The insurance inspectors discovered the hull had been tampered with."

"Abe and Cindy were responsible?" asked Mike.

"Sure thing. It seems they were determined either to hassle their neighbors into giving up their share, or they had just decided that if they couldn't have their way then neither should their neighbors. Anyway, our local sleuths found plenty of evidence that pointed to them, and they eventually confessed.

"Needless to say, it was the end of them with the youth group. All the family connections in the world couldn't save them from the scandal that affair caused. Not that they had the stomach to continue anyway. They resigned within an hour of the police charging them.

"It would be great if I could tell you they made a full repentance and put their trust in the Lord. And it's just possible they did—that's something I won't know this side of eternity. For before the case came to court they had the crash that killed them. They drove through a red light straight into a truck. They died instantly."

Both Bill and Mike stayed in silence for a few moments. Bill, because the memory of the tragedy was still painful to him, and Mike because the seriousness of trifling with the Lord had hit him afresh.

At last Bill broke the silence. The cheerfulness returning to his face. "You know, Mike, for every dark shadow like that God sends a billion sunbeams. Youth work isn't full of tragedy by any means. Come on, let's have one more cup of coffee, and then I'll run you to your apartment. More winners and losers tomorrow.

Chapter 6

The next night Mike arrived at Bill's to find a visitor already there.

"Mike," Bill said, "this is Joe."

A short, dark-haired shy young man came across the room and held out his hand.

"Hi!" he said.

Mike took the offered hand and pumped it vigorously.

"Hello! I heard all about you last night. And it was all good."

"Well, that's a relief," laughed the other.

"Joe's been over most of the day helping me pack. Notice the difference?"

Mike looked around the room and had to admit he couldn't see a great deal of change. If anything, there seemed more half-full boxes and a greater clutter of junk than ever.

Bill and Joe were both grinning.

"The trouble is, when we get together we spend so much time talking, things like packing somehow seem irrelevant," said Bill. "Actually, to be fair to Joe, we would have gotten a lot more done but I was telling him all about last night."

"That's right," Joe confirmed, "and I was just saying to Bill he's made me feel pretty good, putting me in with his winners—alongside Pat, of all people! I'm just not in the same league."

"I think you're a winner alright," said Mike sincerely. "In fact, I wanted to meet you to tell you I got a lot of personal reassurance from your story. I really identified with you."

Joe colored slightly at Mike's appreciative words.

"Thanks, pal!" he said. "But it's only God's grace—and that's not modesty, just the truth."

He decided it was time to move the conversation on to stave off further embarrassment.

"OK—that's enough of me. Now look, Mike, here's what I was suggesting to Bill before you came in. Tonight why don't we look at the winners who could have been losers, and the losers who could have been winners?

"Youth work's crazy, Mike. It's so unpredictable. You might as well be forewarned. Some who had everything stacked against them have come good; others who've had it made have blown it. Like to hear about some?"

"Sounds fine to me," Mike returned.

Bill started towards his beloved computer. "Come on, you guys. Let's get started."

Mike moved to the stool which remained as he'd left it. Joe pulled up an empty packing crate and turned it upside down, flanking Bill on the opposite side from Mike.

The quiet hum of the computer's power supply hinted that everything was ready to roll, and Bill's fingers began to work their magic on the keyboard.

The screen filled with letters.

"Now here's an interesting guy who's causing Joe and me a lot of concern lately—Corky Jones.

The screen announced that Corky was 19, and gave his address and phone number. As always, it was the comments and the biblical code that drew Mike's interest.

"Handsome, strong-minded but slightly shy; can be erratic. A true faith, which is sometimes inconsistent. Inclined to jealousy. *Sa.*"

"With a description like that, *Sa* can only stand for Saul—the Old Testament one, not the New Testament," volunteered Mike.

"Right again," said Bill. He turned to his lieutenant. "Joe, you have a true Bible scholar to work with."

Joe nodded. "I don't doubt it. I hope you're a master psychologist, too, Mike, because there's a lot about Corky I've never really understood."

Mike picked up his Bible from the floor where it lay by his foot, and said, "If he's like Saul I'm not surprised, 'cause I've always found him a bit of a puzzle. Is he a 'goodie' or a 'baddie'? He seems to have so many points to admire, but he goes wrong somewhere. Is that how Corky is?"

"We figure that's where he's heading," Joe replied. "But I'm hoping he'll learn some lessons and come good again. Let me fill you in on his background.

"Corky and me more or less started the youth group together. We'd both been brought up in the church. The only difference is that my folks were here but Corky's never came.

"He was always quite an impressive figure; tall, handsome, athletic. He literally parallels Saul in that the Bible describes him as 'an impressive young man without equal among the Israelites—a head taller than any of the others' (1 Sam. 9:2). I think because of that, right from the start people always tended to look to him for leadership."

"If I can butt in a minute," Mike said, "it's a funny thing, but isn't it true people always tend to put tallness as a criterion for leadership. Our language gives the game away with phrases like 'looking up' to some one and 'head and shoulders above the rest.' But it doesn't always follow that height means leadership ability. I remember when I started high school the teacher picked the tallest boy to be captain. He was such a disaster he got chucked out of the job the first term."

"When you've been in the job as long as I have you'll learn never to go by appearances," said Bill. "Look at Joe here—Mr. Shorty himself."

Joe let the comment pass and picked up his previous thread of conversation. "I think one of the points God was making in choosing Saul as king was that, if the Israelites wanted things done, like having a king, according to ordinary human reasoning, then they should go the whole way and have the one that looked the best. But what a mistake they were making!"

Mike had been thumbing his way through his Bible. "God was pretty upset with them for wanting a king at all, wasn't He? It says here in 1 Samuel 8:7 that God told Samuel that, in asking for a king, Israel hadn't so much rejected Samuel as they had rejected Him."

Joe took up his story again.

"Corky was very popular, and there was a lot of pressure for him to be put into responsibility. But to be fair to him, he was quite modest about his looks and his achievements, which again is true to type with Saul. Because if you look a little further on in your Bible, you'll come to the place where Saul is made king and he couldn't be found because he was hiding in the baggage."

Mike had already found the place in 1 Samuel 10:22.

"Maybe," muttered Bill, looking around at the surrounding chaos, "if he had as much baggage as I've got here he just couldn't disentangle himself in time."

Ignoring this unlikely biblical exegesis, Joe carried on. "In time, the pressure from the group was such that there didn't really seem much option. This was before I got involved in leadership. In fact, I was one of the chief ones who wanted to see Corky on the youth council."

"That's right," Bill added, "and if I might say so, another fine mess you got me into, Stanley." His mimicry of Ollie Hardy was superb. He went on, more seriously. "To be fair, everyone thought he was ideal so we made him secretary. Remember, Mike, the bad time I was having over Kurt? Well, as a result there was a bit of dissatisfaction concerning me in the group, as I think I told you. It seemed to me that if someone as popular as Corky became secretary it would help a lot. And for a time it worked well. Would you say that, Joe, being one of the proletariat at the time?"

"Definitely," agreed Joe. "He was efficient; he didn't shirk anything—he was doing well. But there were flaws in his character biding their time till he was put under stress.

"The first thing that went wrong was the affair of the Taylorsville outreach."

"What was that?" asked Mike.

Bill took up the story. "It was a youth witness project we

were booked to carry out in a neighboring town, based on one of our sister churches. I had planned it with Corky and he had gone over with the six other mission team members to do some preparatory work. I'd arranged to join them on a certain day to start the actual door-to-door visiting. Now they were all raw, young, kids, and I gave Corky strict instructions not to start out before I got there. I wanted to have time to pray with them, help them get oriented—above all, to encourage them in the Lord. I knew that some of them were scared stiff. They'd never done anything like this before.

"Well, just as I was about to drive out of the garage to go over to Taylorsville, someone comes running over and knocks on my windshield. It was an urgent message that another of our kids had been rushed to the hospital. I had to go over there right away. Thankfully, it all turned out OK. But by the time I left the hospital I was late—and I mean late. I didn't have a number to call in Taylorsville so all I could do was go there as fast as I could.

"When I reached the church where the team was camping down, it was already dark. I breezed in with loads of apologies to say it didn't matter that we'd be starting a day late, when what do I find but Corky has taken the team out on his own. Some of them were shattered by the experience. They just weren't ready to go out cold like that.

"I really blew my top with Corky. I'd given him strict instructions and he just hadn't obeyed them. He'd let himself be panicked into a rash action. That was when I made a mental note to put that *Sa* on his file."

"Because you found it reminiscent of Saul's reaction when Samuel was late for the sacrifice?" asked Mike.

"That's right," Bill agreed. "I think that incident in 1 Samuel 13 gives us a red flashing warning light about the weakness of Saul's leadership. He just didn't know how to truly tune in with God.

"The other incident in Saul's life that led me to link his name with Corky's over the Taylorsville affair is that time he fought the Amalekites. Though I can never fully understand the terrible slaughter the Lord commanded there, the message that comes out at the end is plain as the Statue of Liberty on a sunny day. It is that when the Lord says something, you've got to do it and not pretend something else will suffice."

Mike turned to 1 Samuel 15 and noticed the ominous heading in his *NIV*: 'The Lord Rejects Saul as King.' He ran his eye down the column and noted how Saul tried to justify his sparing of the Amalekite sheep on the grounds of their being for the Lord's sacrifices. He paused at verse 22 and read out loud: 'To obey is better than sacrifice, and to heed is better than the fat of rams.'

"It's amazing how we can find good spiritual reasons for our disobedience, isn't it?" Joe said. "I remember once how God tried to convince me to give up a Saturday job that was getting in the way of my Sunday School lesson preparation. And I tried to tell the Lord if I kept the job I'd give Him *half* the money I earned instead of the usual tenth. It didn't work! I had no peace until I gave in."

Bill picked up the threads of Corky's story again. "I know it sounds as though I'm making a lot of that Taylorsville affair, but it was just typical of the kind of rash thing he would do from time to time. He was, and still is, a true believer and I like him a lot, but he just seems out of touch with God and acts from human impulse rather than real spiritual insight."

"But we all make mistakes," Mike objected. "None of us gets it right all the time."

"True; but it's more a general attitude and lack of God-awareness I'm thinking of," Bill went on.

"Still, we sorted things out, and life in the youth group went on. The Kurt business ended and everything seemed to be going well. But then new clouds blew up on the horizon, and the cause of them is sitting not three feet from you."

"Sir," sid Joe, rising from his packing case and bowing with mock solemnity towards Mike, "let me introduce myself. Mr. Cumulus Nimbus, as dark a storm cloud as ever blackened a sky."

"What did you do wrong?" asked Mike, raising his eyebrows in exaggerated surprise.

"It wasn't what I did *wrong* so much as what he did *right*," said Bill. "This is where we see another Sauline trait (if that's the right word) surfacing in Corky. You see, I was just beginning to notice those gifts in Joe which, as I told you last night but which I won't repeat for fear of making his head swell, made me believe God wanted him drawn into the leadership of our group. I started out by giving Joe little jobs to do, just to see how he responded. And I liked everything I saw. I took Corky into my confidence about Joe and I must admit that I was deeply hurt and shocked by his reaction—it was sheer, unvarnished jealousy. It was so nakedly blatant that even some of the kids in the group noticed it. It was just like the way Saul resented David."

"So Joe is a David as well as a Timothy?" said Mike. He couldn't resist picturing the mild, shy Joe in a loin cloth swirling a sling around his head, ready to bring down Goliath.

"Ah, yes," said Joe, "I'm a man of many parts. Don't forget, I'm a storm cloud too!"

Bill ignored the frivolous treatment of his analysis and carried on talking. "In the Bible's account of Saul, that jealousy gets really extreme, so that the king starts throwing spears to kill David. Fortunately, he's a rotten shot. I don't want to give the wrong impression—Corky has never done anything like that. But you know that Jesus said if you are angry with your brother you are liable to judgment as much as a murderer (Matt. 5:21,22). Corky began to say some very hurtful things both to Joe and to me about Joe. He was slaying him with words."

"What sort of things?" asked Mike.

"He would criticize me a lot," said Joe. "Given my insecure nature and the fact I'd never wanted to be a leader anyway . . ."

". . . which was one of the main reasons why I thought he'd be such a good one," chipped in Bill.

"As I was saying, not wanting to be a leader and feeling very inadequate, it didn't take much to make me feel absolutely terrible. I got depressed, I tried to get Bill to agree to my giving up. It was lousy."

Bill said, "I didn't let him give up because I knew that would be giving in to the devil. But things were very awkward. Yet at the same time I didn't want to lose Corky. He had so many good qualities. I spent hours with him, trying to counsel him and help him see he must put the Lord and His glory first. Jealousy is such a tenacious weed, though. Once you let it take root, it won't give up easily."

Mike's mind's eye conjured up the home he had left in England, with its garden wall and the profusion of red valerian growing out of it. Quite an attractive, colorful flower, but he remembered his unsuccessful attempts to get rid of it. Breaking off the stems did no good. It would only sprout up somewhere else, and all the time its roots were mining their way through the mortar until the stones began to drop out. Eventually, the whole wall collapsed. And he remembered, too, his own feelings of envy at his school friends getting higher marks than he, and at the Bible college classmate who had become assistant at one of the largest churches in Britain. (He didn't know that this same classmate was extremely envious that Mike had made it to America.) Yes, thought Mike, envy is a very pernicious weed indeed. No wonder Paul, in Galatians 5:19-21, listed it with acts of the evil nature, including idolatry.

"What's the answer?" Mike felt impelled to ask. "After all, you don't invite those feelings in, do you? They just come when you're least expecting them."

Bill's chunky frame swung around on his chair to face Mike. "We all have a problem in this area, because jealousy is just one species of the basic cause of all our troubles—namely, self. And I think we've all discovered it's no good trying to pretend we're not envious. It doesn't work. Deny the feeling one time and it will pop up another, as strong as ever."

Mike thought of his red valerian again, and his attempts to pull it out by hand.

Bill went on, "I've found two things help me most. The first is not to deny it, but to admit it and then to disown it. I think of that verse in Romans 7:17—a passage, incidentally, which shows that Paul had exactly the same problem as us."

Mike quickly turned to the verse Bill named and followed it with his eye as Bill quoted it from memory.

"'It is no longer I myself who do it, but it is sin living in me.' That means it belongs to the old nature of pre-conversion days."

"The old man who's dead but won't lie down," Joe added helpfully.

"Right," said Bill, "that doesn't mean I ignore my responsibility. The sin is mine, and mine alone, and so I must repent and ask God's forgiveness. But I'm saying it has no right to be part of me anymore. I take authority over it, in a manner of speaking.

"Then the second thing is to starve it to death. We have the Holy Spirit because we are Christians, which sets us free from the treadmill of envy. So we should direct our attention positively towards the things of the Spirit. I don't mean in some airy-fairy way, but practically.

"For example, suppose I'm envious of Jim, our present pastor here at Fairmont. Instead of getting all burned up about it, I'll go out of my way to pray for him more, to do him good."

"Suppose the person you're envious of is a louse?" Joe asked.

"All the more reason to take that positive attitude," said Bill emphatically. "'If your enemy is hungry, feed him; if he is thirsty, give him something to drink,' to quote just one text on the subject, Romans 12:20."

"What about Corky?" Mike inquired.

Bill looked sad. "He did the very opposite of all I've been saying. He fed his envy and jealousy. He didn't even have the excuse that Saul had of being mentally unbalanced. It was plain, downright sin."

Joe broke in, "I think the most hurtful thing was when I won a Bible knowledge competition in our denominational magazine. He made all kinds of innuendoes that I had cheated. None of the mud stuck, but it was sure upsetting at the time."

"What's Corky's position now?" Mike wanted to know, partly from fearfulness at having such an awkward customer in his squad.

"Well, he's still with us," Bill replied, "but he's no longer secretary. He resigned a year or so ago in a huff because I sent Joe as our delegate to a national youth congress."

Bill shrugged his huge shoulders in a sigh.

"We've tried hard enough with him, goodness only knows. I've encouraged him, rebuked him, counseled him, prayed with him and for him, all to no avail. I think a lot of the problem is his preoccupation with his self-image and what he thinks people think of him. Just like Saul."

"How do you mean?" Mike questioned.

"Well, let's go back to 1 Samuel 9 where Samuel first finds Saul."

Mike found the spot. Bill leaned over, turned the Bible around to face him, and ran his finger down the page.

"Look here at verse 21. See how he says he is from the smallest tribe of Israel, and his clan is the least of that tribe. Yet the first two verses . . . " he ran his finger up the page. " . . . here, say that his father was 'a man of standing . . . ' and that Saul was 'without equal among the Israelites.' That speaks to me of a man with a huge sense of inferiority—a very insecure man who can't believe his true worth. That seems to be born out by his antics when he was made king, how he hid among the baggage, remember?"

"But I thought we'd put that down to modesty, a good trait?" Mike objected.

"Modesty *can* be a good trait, if it comes out of a genuine desire to let God have the glory and because you've risen above natural pride. But often, it comes out of sheer funk, because you're afraid of not being able to deliver the goods. It can actually be a cloak for pride, woven out of the threads of our self-doubt."

Mike wasn't too sure about the soundness of Bill's analysis but let him continue.

"Now in the matter of his premature sacrifice at Gilgal in chapter 13, I think that shows Saul's basic insecurity as well. He panicked. In the same way, when there was that stupid affair of banning his soldiers from eating and drinking during the long hard battle in chapter 14, it seems to me he was trying desperately to impress God and twist His arm to give a victory."

Joe was the one to interrupt this time. "But I get the impression that Saul, for all his faults, was a very brave man. Think of all the battles he fought. How about the time he rescued the city of Jabesh, for example?" He flicked the page of Mike's Bible back to chapter 11 and swept his hand demonstratively down the page.

"That may be so," Bill responded, undeterred. "But many,

many times outward bravery can conceal the most dreadful inner uncertainty. There is more than one kind of courage, and the more obvious sort is not necessarily the highest. Brave in battle, Saul couldn't stand up to 'people pressure.' He just caved in, as he admits in 1 Samuel 15:24. I believe Saul was never *really* sure of God, and that was the problem. He tried to please Him, true, but when the crunch came, he plainly wasn't 100 percent convinced."

"Are you thinking of his visit to the medium at Endor?" asked Mike.

"I am indeed," said Bill. "Check out chapter 28."

Mike found it.

"Now see what it says in verse 3. 'Saul had expelled the mediums and spiritists from the land.' This was obviously no half-hearted measure because this one remaining medium was in fear for her life."

Bill pointed to verse 9. "And yet here he was asking for help from her. A last resort, maybe, but in view of his previous uncompromising attitude, he ought never to have been there at all. Now do you see what I mean about Saul being unsure of himself and unsure of the Lord?"

"I do, I do," Mike emphasized. "I still can't help feeling sorry for Saul, though—a man who never asked to be king in the first place, who showed so much promise, a man who came to such a dreadful end committing suicide on the battlefield. You don't think Corky will finish like that, do you?"

"Mike," said Bill, "this job you're starting isn't possible unless you have hope. Let's trust he'll come good. You start praying, I'll carry on praying, Joe'll start praying—let's see what God can do."

Chapter 7

"Coffee's up!"
Once more the geriatric coffee machine had done its faithful best, and with a gurgle and a sputter the dark brown liquid gradually filled the jug.

Bill moved over to the table and began filling the three mugs.

"Anyone want something to eat? Sandwich? Cookie? Sorry, Mike—I mean biscuit."

"You wouldn't have a nice packet of chips wrapped in newspaper, would you?" the Englishman sighed, thinking nostalgically of the corner shop back home.

"Uh-uh," Bill shook his head.

"Then a cookie will have to do."

"It just so happens . . . " Joe began to say, only to be interrupted by a joyful snort from an elated Bill.

"You don't mean she's . . . "

"She has!"

Mike looked utterly baffled at the other two's exaltation.

"What's going on?" he asked, looking from one to the other, bemused.

"Friend, you are just about to be initiated into the greatest . . . " Bill began.

"Not to say the fruitiest . . . " interposed Joe.

"And the tangiest. In fact the flavorfullest taste in the whole

U.S. of A.!" concluded Bill, lifting his hand in a smart salute.

With a "ta-raa!" mock trumpet call, Joe went over to where his discarded windbreaker lay on the floor. He whisked it up in the air to reveal a round tin which he picked up and brought back to where Mike was sitting, who by now had the steaming coffee in his hands.

"This," began Joe, maintaining the air of mystery, "is what we're talking about. Georgina's cookies."

"I'd better explain," Bill offered. "Georgina is Joe's girlfriend. Go on Joe—open sesame."

Joe pulled the lid off like a jeweler about to show his most precious gem to a customer, and there in the opened container Mike saw the most delectable, desirable, and utterly consumable examples of patisserie artistry he had ever seen. The variety of pastries, shortcakes, and other confectionary looked and smelled so good he felt the saliva begin to flow in his mouth as impatient taste buds jumped to send urgent messages demanding action. Faced with such delicate delights, thoughts of fish and chips seemed positively indecent and faded quickly from his mind.

As Mike gratefully plucked one of the delicious cookies from the proffered tin, he said, "If Georgina can cook like this, and the way to a man's heart is through his stomach, no wonder you're going out with her. I'm only sorry you got here before me."

"Cooking isn't the only thing that's nice about her." Joe's enthusiastic words betrayed how badly smitten he was. Cupid's arrow had buried itself up to its feathers.

"Here's her picture."

Joe fished out his wallet and extracted from it a small colored photo, showing a petite, red-haired girl, with firm but gentle features, whose bright eyes and generous smile enhanced an already beautiful face. He noticed the distinct, confident but feminine handwriting: "To my darling Joe, all my love. Georgina."

"Ten years here and I'm still single," Bill mused with a not totally spurious regret in his voice. "Joe's hardly out of diapers and he gets a girl like Georgina. Ah, well, the Lord knows what He's doing."

Mike was too busy enjoying his third cookie to be over-interested in Bill's continuing bachelorhood.

Between the three of them, the tin rapidly emptied. As the last crumbs were greedily gleaned from the corners of the container, Bill swung around in his chair to face his computer once again.

"That little feast is as good an introduction as I could want for my next file. I'd like to tell you Georgina's story."

He cocked his head left towards Joe.

"You don't mind, do you?"

"No—sure go ahead." Then with a broad grin. "You know me; I'd like to talk about her all the time!"

Bill shook his head in some incomprehension. For all his twinge of regret at his singleness, he felt that computers were a lot easier to handle than women. Once again the electronic device responded to his fingertips and in microseconds the screen was full of data. From it, Mike learned that Georgina's surname was Lafayette, that she was 18, and that her biblical "double," Bill had decided, was *Ab*.

Mike studied the section marked "Comments" to try to guess what the enigmatic initials might mean. He read: Pleasant, popular, attractive girl. No hang-ups. Gentle but strong and decisive. Integrity 100 percent. Peacemaker. Wise. Difficult background.

Mike pondered long and hard before he spoke, Joe and Bill waiting for his reply with expectant smiles. At last he broke his silence.

"That's certainly some description. She's obviously going to be one of the really good people in the Bible, but who? *Ab* . . . humm . . . no, I give in."

"Abigail," said Bill. Then, seeing Mike still looked a bit mystified, he added, "in the story of David, you know she became one of David's wives."

"First Samuel 25," Joe interjected, who knew the reference by heart, having Bill's file engraved rather specially in his mind.

Mike turned to the chapter at once and thoughtfully read it to himself, the Fairmont youth pastor and his assistant waiting while he did.

At last Mike lifted his head.

"Yes, I remember it now. It's certainly a fine story and I can see how what you've written on the screen fits the description of Abigail here in this chapter. But is there a deeper reason for linking Georgina with her? After all, she is one of the minor characters of the Bible—and Georgina is pretty important to at least one of us."

He gave a knowing wink in Joe's direction, but it was Bill who took up the question.

"I'm not sure the amount of space God has given to people in the Scripture is a measure of their importance. But leaving that aside, the answer is yes—there are parallels between Abigail and Georgina that aren't immediately obvious from that screen.

"Let's begin with the background first. Will you tell it, Joe, or shall I?"

Joe nodded towards Bill as a signal for him to carry on.

"OK. Well, we have here another problem parent case. You remember Kurt and his dad from last night? Georgina's dad was from the same mold as Kurt's but the big difference is that, whereas Kurt followed in his father's footsteps, Georgina turned out quite differently from hers, which in itself was a miracle. She was unfortunate enough to lose her mom to cancer when she was three and so for almost as long as she can remember she was brought up by her dad and a succession of paid baby-sitters. She's come to church since she was little—her mom started her off before she died and after that I think Mr. Lafayette just found it a convenient way to get rid of her for a whole Sunday morning to be left alone with his booze."

"Is he an alcoholic, then?" asked Mike.

"Not quite, but a very, very heavy drinker," Bill replied.

Joe butted in with some passion: "An alcoholic is often the death of himself; Lafayette's heavy drinking left him with enough sense to be almost the death of Georgina."

"How do you mean?" Mike wanted to know.

"Violence," Joe rapped out with still greater warmth of feeling. "He used to beat her. I don't mean ordinary fatherly discipline, but really vindictive thrashings over the most trivial things. Sometimes for nothing at all."

"Did that have no bad effect on her?" asked Mike. "I remember our pastor back home telling me once that he had to help dozens of problem people over the years who had been marred by over-zealous corporal punishment in the home or in school."

Joe replied, his voice calmer now. "Amazing as it seems, Georgina grew up sweet as honey. I can't explain it apart from a miracle. However, the one thing that I think was affected was her response to the Lord. As nice a girl as she was, she didn't accept the Lord until quite recently—just about six months ago in fact. And that was in spite of hearing the gospel from the time she was tiny, and in spite of having a youth pastor like Bill."

"It takes the Holy Spirit to convict and convert," Bill said quietly, a mild rebuke in his tone.

"Nevertheless, I believe the rough treatment her father handed out held her back from Christian commitment. What she has told me is that all the talk of God as Father left her cold. In fact it frightened her to death. Just to start the Lord's Prayer and say 'Our Father' meant for her a mental image of an ogre with a big stick."

Mike still had his Bible open at 1 Samuel 25, and as Joe was speaking, he was re-reading the ancient story. He decided to interrupt again.

"Joe, I'm really fascinated by what you're telling me, but I'm not sure how this fits in with Abigail. As far as I can see, her father doesn't even come into the story."

Bill spoke for Joe, wanting to defend his computer system.

"Be patient, Mike. We're talking about general parallels with this idea of spiritual doubles. You won't get exact equivalents from then to now. It would be unrealistic to expect them. But have a look at Abigail's husband, Nabal. Don't you find him close in kind to Georgina's dad? Verse 3, for example, describes him as 'surly and mean.' And his servants had a somewhat low view of him. They describe him in verse 17 as 'such a wicked man that no one can talk with him,' while Abigail herself tells David in verse 25 that her husband really is a 'fool,' just like the meaning of his name, Nabal. On top of that, he shares with Georgina's father a liking for the bottle. We find him in verse 36 'very drunk.' But there's even more to tie the two stories up if you'll only be patient and hear Joe out."

"Oh, I want to hear, alright. Carry on, Joe, please."

"Well," said Joe, "of course a lot of what went on in the Lafayette household was unknown to us. Georgina is so loyal. She wouldn't give her dad away, ever. We guessed from what we knew of his general character that Georgina couldn't exactly be having a great time. Like we read about Nabal, he was surly and mean. He never had a good word for anyone, and he was a real tightwad."

Suddenly Joe's face broke into a grin.

"I'll never forget the time we sent Corky around when he was still secretary to ask for a donation for our youth wing fund. He came back, his face as white as a sheet, and said he'd heard words he never knew existed before."

Joe resumed the story.

"Anyway, we never knew just how badly he'd treated Georgina through the years.

"She was about 14 when I first got interested in dating her. But I was so shy I didn't like to ask her out. In fact it was a whole year before I got the nerve to do it."

"Slow starter, fast finisher," Bill added good-humoredly.

Joe continued, undeterred by the interruption.

"I used to see her home on our dates, but she would never ask me in, which hurt me a little bit. Being so insecure, I couldn't help thinking she was a bit ashamed of me. Now I'm ashamed of ever thinking that of her. She was just trying to protect me from her dad because she knew there would be fireworks if I were with him for more than five minutes. He'd made it pretty clear to Georgina that he didn't think much of any of us church kids."

"Did she tell you about her father abusing her?" asked Mike.

"No, like I said, she was absolutely loyal. The first clue I had was when we went swimming together once. (She was about 16 at the time.) We were lying facedown on the poolside sunbathing. I happened to look up and I noticed these blue bruises on the back of both legs. It didn't click with me then how they had been caused. I asked her, of course, but she put me off with something about falling off her bike. I must admit it sounded unlikely, but I couldn't press it any further.

"Our relationship went on developing real great so that all

the kids were dropping hints, sometimes not very subtle, that it was about time we got engaged."

Bill couldn't resist interrupting with some relish.

"Like one Valentine's night the group all pretended to book a group meal at Rico's Restaurant. When Joe and Georgina arrived they found they were the only ones who actually had a table reserved—complete with candles, soft music, and a heart-shaped cake for dessert. No one else from the group turned up until right at the end when they all burst through the door singing 'Congratulations.' Fortunately, the manager is a friend of ours."

"Did it work?" asked Mike.

"No, sir!" said Joe with emphasis enough to drill an oil well. "We were just plain embarrassed. Anyway, apart from anything else, although I was sure I was in love, I wasn't quite sure about Georgina. She still seemed secretive about her home life and although by then I was getting into her home, my relationship with Mr. Lafayette was still fairly precarious. And though she believed in the Lord after a fashion, there was a vital spark missing in Georgina's spiritual experience. However much I loved Georgina, I believed with all my heart—and still do—the Lord must come first."

"Another reason why I picked Joe for my assistant," interposed Bill quickly. Joe colored up slightly once more and hurried on with the story.

"Then about a year ago something happened that brought everything to a crisis. We'd been out to a church barbecue and one of the kids, in fun, had jacked up my car in the parking lot and had taken two wheels off and hidden them. Well, in the dark, it took about an hour to find them and we started back real late."

"Having also lost a little time finding the culprit and covering his face with barbecue sauce," added Bill, in the interest of truth, the whole truth, and nothing but the truth.

"All in good fun, you understand," said Joe, the twinkle in his eye betraying that he still enjoyed the mental picture of the tire-thief's ketchup-anointed face. He chuckled as he remembered how he'd sat astride the poor guy's chest while Georgina had squeezed the polyethylene bottle with delight.

But the seriousness of what he was about to tell made the twinkle fade and the chuckle subside.

"It was about 11:30 when we got back to her house. I asked Georgina if she wanted me to see her in but she assured me all would be well and it would be better if I just drove off as quickly and quietly as I could, which I did. I wasn't happy about it, knowing her father the little I did. If I'd known him just an inch better though, I wouldn't have driven off for a million bucks. In fact, I wouldn't have let Georgina go back at all.

"The next day was Saturday, and in spite of my uneasiness the night before, I slept late and didn't get up until my mom called up the stairs to say that one of our gang from the church was there and wanted me urgently. I grabbed my pants and my shirt and threw them on as fast as I could, and came down to find Don, who lives next door to Georgina, looking very worried.

"It's about Georgina," he said, and he went on to explain how when we'd arrived at her house last night he was still up, though he'd gotten home about an hour before. He had heard me drive off and he'd heard Georgina's door click shut. But what he heard next had scared him silly. Georgina's father seemed to be going berserk. He could hear so much shouting. After a few minutes he could bear it no longer, and went to his side window to look across to Lafayette's house. He was horrified to see in the uncurtained window opposite that beast of a man laying about Georgina with his hands, slapping her, punching her, with the girl trying to defend herself as best she could. He could see as well the empty beer cans on the table. Don didn't know what to do, but was building up his courage to run across when suddenly Georgina's dad gave up and stormed off. The next thing he heard was a door slam and after that nothing. Presumably Lafayette had gone to his own bedroom. Georgina herself moved out of the line of sight of the window, so Don wasn't sure what her state was, nor did he know what to do next. He didn't think going across then would help; in fact, it might make matters worse. So he decided that unless Georgina came running out for help, he would just have to leave things till morning, which was what he had done, hence his visit to me.

"You can imagine how I felt. My immediate reaction was to

storm over and smash up that monster. I mean, I know as a Christian I ought to forgive, but it's much harder to forgive someone for harming your dearest love than it is to forgive him for hurting you. It was at that moment of burning anger I realized just how much I did care for Georgina.

"Then it burst on me like a delayed-action mine that I didn't have any idea what Georgina's condition was. Was she injured? Had something been broken? I rushed out to the hall and grabbed the phone and spun the dial so fast it almost flew off like a Frisbee. To my relief, Georgina answered. At least she was alive. I poured into that phone mouthpiece a torrent of questions, anxieties, threats about her dad, and I don't know what. When she got a moment to get a word in, she was as calm as a New England fall. 'Now, hold on Joe. Don't you come charging over here. You stay right where you are and I'll come and see you as soon as I can.'

"I had to agree, although all my instincts were still to go over with clenched fists—if not a baseball bat—and really give that tomcat a lesson.

"Don left and I spent the next few minutes pacing up and down in my room waiting. At last Georgina arrived. I had the door open as soon as I saw her at the end of the street. I almost tore her coat from her to see if I could see bruises on her arm. Her face had one or two minor blue marks though my agitation at the time magnified them to near fatal injuries.

"Once all the initial exchanges of words were over, we sat down on the couch. But I was still seething inside. I began to say what I was planning. The first thing was she had to move out. The second was I would confront her father and tell him why. The third was that I was going to report him for assault. I wasn't sure who to report him to, the police or what, and I didn't know how to go about it, but I was determined to do it and I didn't care how much he hated me or threatened me; I'd stand up in court and tell all the world about him."

"This is our shy Timothy, remember?" said Bill to Mike. "Not much spirit of fear there, eh?"

"Wrong story, Bill," smiled Mike. "This is David, the fearless warrior!"

"It just shows we're not limited to our natural temperament all our lives. God *can* make the weak strong. But I mustn't interrupt. Carry on, Joe."

"Well, when Georgina responded to my three-fold plan I was utterly amazed. I expected she would need convincing, but I felt that her safety, my honor, and God's justice were all at stake. So I was determined to get her to agree with me. But I was absolutely stunned by her calm attitude—and her absolute wisdom. Talk about clear thinking.

"She explained to me how throughout the years her father had always had periodic bursts of cruelty towards her, usually when he was on one of his drinking bouts. But lately, as she had grown older, he had gotten better. So the last night had been right out of the blue.

"Then she dealt with my proposals one by one. First, she couldn't move out because she believed that at least until she was 18 she was committed to care for her father. With no woman in the house, how would he cope? She quoted the command 'Honor your father and your mother.' Second, if I confronted her father, would we ever be friends? She wanted me to help bring her dad to a better way of life. How could I do that if I took her away like that? As for the third thing, well, she just looked me straight in the eye and said, 'Joe, if you even threaten such a thing again, I'll never speak to you for ever!' And then she just burst into tears."

Joe looked a bit sheepish as he added "I must admit I wept a bit too.

"The thing was," he continued, "that she desperately wanted to be loyal to her father, in spite of him being so rotten to her. And I also came to see that just as desperately she did not want me to do anything that would spoil me. The only person she wasn't considering very much was herself."

"I see what you mean by making her an Abigail," said Mike. He looked at his still-open Bible. "She saved Nabal's household from death, and she saved David from shedding blood and the guilt he would have incurred as a result. Two ladies in the same mold. What's the situation now with Georgina?"

"The wedding date's fixed," said Joe, a huge Grand Canyon

of a smile splitting his face. "Six months' time—you're invited."

"Thanks a lot, I'll be there. But what about your reservations over Georgina's spiritual state?"

"Well, all this trouble drove us together, real close, and now her secret about her dad's treatment of her was out. She became absolutely open with me and a new sort of tenderness came into our relationship. She says that through that she came to realize what love is. If I loved her and it felt so good, how much greater God's love must be. So six months ago, when we were alone after a meeting, she said, 'Joe, you know I've never really invited Jesus to take over my life completely. I guess my problem at home gave me a bit of a chip on my shoulder and I couldn't really trust God to love me. But I can now. I want to ask Jesus in. Will you help me?' 'You bet!' I said. Mike, it was the most wonderful time in my whole Christian experience."

Mike was quite carried away by Joe's moving account. Not the romantic type himself, he generally preferred reading sports and adventure books to the love and kisses stuff. But this was something else. He felt almost weepy.

He was brought back to earth by a stern-sounding Bill.

"Of course, I generally discourage teenage marriages. In fact, I came as close as I can to forbidding them altogether in the youth group. Experience has shown me they hardly ever last. The divorce rate is horrifying."

Then suddenly his face was all sunshine.

"But this is one tremendous exception."

"What makes you think so?" Mike was curious to know.

"Well, leaving aside the calibre of our present company for the moment, I just am so bowled over by Georgina's strength of character. She's a real peacemaker who has discovered that peacemaking is not a cowardly easy option, but the most costly exercise on earth. It takes more guts and resolution to be a peacemaker than it ever does to be the great revolutionary stirring up hornets' nests everywhere. Not that there aren't times for being on the offensive and that sometimes you have to go out and make a nuisance of yourself in the Lord's name. But all I'm saying is that peacemaking can be the more difficult thing."

"I guess you're right," said Mike thoughtfully. "After all, it cost Jesus the cross. However . . . " he hesitated, frowning slightly.

" . . . I can't help being bothered by the thought that Georgina's father got off scot-free from his dreadful treatment of his daughter."

"Mike," said Bill, "there are many people in this world who seem to escape any punishment for their evil deeds, but on the authority of God's Word I can assure you solemnly that no one, but no one, ever really gets off scot-free. Our God is a holy, just God and this is a moral universe. Sometimes we see that proven in the way people get their just desserts here and now. That is exactly what happened to Abigail's first husband who died very suddenly you'll remember. For others, judgment waits, but eternity will sort out all the injustices, believe me. And let's remember that text '"It is mine to avenge; I will repay," says the Lord.'"

"But there're a couple of other things as far as we Christians are concerned. One is that none of us dare judge someone else, because we are all condemned in God's sight. We're all sinners, and we're saved by God's grace alone. If Jesus hadn't soaked up the consequences of our sin, we'd be lost, just as much condemned as any murderer.

"The other thing is that we surely have got to believe no one is beyond the reach of God's grace. The real test of whether we're genuine peacemakers or just spineless peace-at-any-price jerks is how seriously we'll pray for the Lafayettes of this world, that they'll find salvation too."

"That's right," said Joe. "That's what Georgina has taught me. Peacemakers are positive people."

Chapter 8

After the Georgina saga Joe went off to an appointment. Mike didn't think he needed to ask with whom. Meanwhile, Bill had been punching the keys of his micro and bringing to the screen a rapid succession of youth group members, giving Mike a brief biography of each with constant reference to Bible characters. Some were well-known, others barely remembered by anyone but the most diligent Scripture students.

Suddenly he swung around in his swivel chair. "Tell me the first word you think of when I say this name: Uriah."

"Heep," fired back Mike immediately.

Bill roared with delight. "I guessed it! I knew you'd say that. An Englishman who knows his Dickens. Now tell me what the name conjures up in your mind."

"Somebody slimy—a toady, a backscratcher, unctuous, always grovelling . . . "

"Hold on there!" Bill yelled. "You sound like a thesaurus. But you're absolutely right. That's Uriah Heep alright. You know, Charles Dickens had such a wonderful gift for picking descriptive names for his characters that you can't ever imagine people being anything other than what they are in his books. The trouble is, that fixes the name in a permanent pigeon-hole in your mind. And that's a great shame with the name Uriah. Like you, I only have to hear it to think immediately of a real creep—a totally repugnant non-person. But in the Bible, the real Uriah is one of the most attractive people in the whole book. Brave, loyal, true; he's magnificent."

Bill swiveled around on his chair to man his computer once more.

"In fact, I want us to look at someone from our youth group that to me is a true Uriah."

Mike watched the screen as Bill faultlessly executed the keyboard operation and he found himself gazing at a block of electronic print that said, "Bob Williams, Age 22. Address: 627 Charles Street. Tel: 554-9320. Comments: soundly converted. Honest, great integrity. Dogged perseverance. Courageous witness. Holds up under trial"—followed, naturally, by the code letters *Ur.*"

With the exploits Mike had had recounted to him that night and the night before, he was eager to hear Bob's story, but Bill wanted Mike to refresh his mind about the sad case of Uriah from the Bible. Mike turned to 2 Samuel, chapter 11, and read it through. As with every previous occasion he had read the passage, he felt anger bristling inside him at David's callous and cold-blooded actions. He expressed his rankle to Bill.

"Well you're not the only one, I guess," the youth pastor replied. "The last thing the chapter says is 'the thing David had done displeased the Lord.' It just shows that no one is immune from temptation, not even us youth pastors! However, I don't want to get into David's crime and all that followed. It's Uriah, the poor, innocent victim we're concentrating on. What do you make of him, Mike?"

"Seems to me you hit the nail on the head, Bill, with your description a few minutes ago. A man who's absolutely loyal and true. A straight iron rod who won't bend, snap, or melt under any pressure or heat."

"Sounds like the archetypal Englishman," said Bill with friendly irony in his voice.

"Oh, we've got plenty of bent people back home, don't you worry. But talking of nationality, that's one thing that impresses me about Uriah here." Mike tapped his finger on the third verse of the chapter. "He is a Hittite, not an Israelite. So here you have a man who is not one of the Lord's people living righteously, while the man who is not only the Lord's but has a very special calling, living like a heathen."

Mike shook his head. "It doesn't really make sense," he said.

"I think you'll have a lot of puzzles like that in your career as a youth pastor," Bill replied. "But don't ever use them as an excuse to sell the Lord short yourself. Keep your eye on God and leave the other fella for God to deal with Himself. Now, what more about Uriah?"

Mike studied the passage again.

"Seems to me that his faithfulness is no temporary effort. He's absolutely consistent. On the first night back from the battle line he refuses to sleep with his wife, contrary to David's wishes, who wants to cover his own adultery with her. But he shows the same resolution the second night and that, in spite of David trying to dissolve his resistance with alcohol, well that really shows the mettle of the man."

"I agree absolutely," Bill said, "and those are exactly the qualities that our friend Bob has.

"Bob came to us when he was 16, right out of the blue. His folks had absolutely no connection with ours or any other church. In fact, though they didn't bother to think their position through, they would probably have described themselves as agnostics. Typical shoulder-shrugging, 'Well, it's alright for you, but don't bother me' type of people.

"Bob turned up at one of our recreation nights and simply said, 'I'm not a Christian, but some of your members have been talking to me about Christ at school. I want to know more.'

"Now that's pretty unusual. But I was to find out that was typical of the guy. He just comes straight to the point. No embarrassment, no messing, no gift wrap. So, in about the time it takes to say John 3:16 twice, he'd accepted the Lord and he was away on his Christian adventure. I doubt if he's looked back once.

"Right away, he became a witness. Not the buttonholing 'are-you-saved?' sort, though he certainly had the courage to do that if he believed it was the right approach. But an intelligent, discriminating, witness. Yet he always goes straight to the point—absolutely fearless. I don't know how many he's led to the Lord. You know how Uriah was put into David's special band of 30 mighty men? (2 Sam. 23:39, 1 Chron. 11:41). In a way, that's what I did with Bob. He became part of our trained witness team that goes out all over the state."

"He sounds a winner all the way," said Mike, a little wistfully as he thought of some of his past pathetic attempts at telling others about his faith in Christ.

"I couldn't agree more, and I'm sure that's how God sees him. But there was a little time when he looked like a real loser. In fact, I'm just coming up to that part of his story now.

"For all his evangelistic gift, Bob is not what you would call an academic. So he didn't go to college but instead went to work in a hardware and domestic appliance store across town. The store is managed by a Christian; he doesn't come to our church but I know him well. In fact it was through my contact that Bob got the job. I gave him a really good reference which, as it turned out, was a bit ironic because in the end it wasn't Bob's integrity that needed questioning.

"The job went like a dream, and Bob was very happy. Working in the store, he was meeting people all the time, and that gave him plenty of opportunity to witness. The manager didn't seem to mind at all.

"Then things began to degenerate. As the manager got to know Bob better he seemed to get the idea he could trust him to cheat, if you know what I mean."

"Not sure that I do," Mike said.

"What I mean is that Bob's boss let his front of strict, Christian uprightness slip a little and showed that behind it the truth was crumpled more than somewhat. He appeared to think he was paying Bob a compliment, letting him in on a big secret he was privileged to know.

"Mind you, Bob had had a little inkling by the way that right from the start he'd had to resist the manager's instructions to tell telephone callers he was out when he was in. But Bob knew that was more or less standard in business, so although he wouldn't be party to it, he didn't take too much notice. But he got a bit more worried over what happened when an old lady brought in a vacuum cleaner for repair. It turned out that a wire was loose in the plug. Bob didn't deal with it himself so forgot about it until a couple of weeks later when he was going through the month's bills and found the woman had been charged 20 dollars—just for a loose wire. The bill had been written up to make it look as though something really major had been done.

"Then the boss started initiating Bob in the way to alter price markings, and how to reap a harvest of odd cents that could mount up to a tidy personal profit. Of course, Bob would have none of it, which annoyed his employer greatly and that was when their relationship began to break down. Bob would come and talk to me about it and we would pray together. But there was very little he could do, except look for another job. He wouldn't have dreamt of going behind the manager's back to the owners of the store. Straight as Bob was, he wasn't going to rat on anyone.

"Things tottered on for a few months, and then something devastating happened. One morning, Bob went down to the store to open up and found that the back door had been forced open. He went in and saw the safe door swinging wide. He was shocked and upset, but not overly-bothered. He knew there would only have been about 800 dollars in the safe, the proceeds of last-minute sales after the rest of yesterday's cash had been banked. Nothing else appeared to be touched. It looked a typical small-time robbery, no more than a flea-bite to the fairly substantial company Bob worked for. So Bob did all the right things—got the police, phoned the manager, made his statement, and so on. He then got on with his business as usual, and apart from making a conversation piece, the break-in had very little effect on his life.

"At least that was how it was until a couple of days later when two cops called in the store and said they wanted to talk to him again about the incident. He took them into the office, they sat him down and started a barrage of questions, and it gradually dawned on him that they were treating him as a suspect, not a witness.

"What it all boiled down to was that the manager had gone to the police and told them he was concerned about Bob because there were things he thought incriminated him. He had told them apparently that Bob alone would have known there was anything worth stealing. Usually there was virtually nothing in the safe. Then again, Bob knew the back door could easily be forced, for once when both had arrived without their keys, Bob had gotten in that way. They had never gotten around to strengthening it after that. When Bob objected to the police that he wouldn't have needed to break in because he had a key anyway, they naturally replied that the apparent forced entry was a cover. Most damning of all, they said, was that they could find no evidence the safe lock had been tampered with. It almost certainly had been opened with a key, and they knew he had one.

"Bob was absolutely stunned. But he didn't lose his head. He realized all the evidence was purely circumstantial and was unlikely to carry any chance of success in court, though he dreaded the thought of the slur on his name and wondered how he was ever going to face anybody again, for there will always be those who say 'no smoke without fire.'

"But he didn't know the cops weren't through with him yet. Realizing and expecting he wasn't suddenly going to break down and confess, one of the cops, without warning, demanded to see his wallet.

"Bob, taken by surprise, had a sinking feeling as he did as they asked, though he couldn't think what could possibly be incriminating about it. However, when he handed it to the cop he saw the man fan through all his bills and suddenly with a shout of triumph pull out a 20-dollar bill and wave it under Bob's nose, meanwhile tapping his forefinger of his other hand accusingly into Bob's chest.

"'OK, Mr. Clean, how come this is in your possession?'

"Poor Bob didn't know what to make of it. He didn't have a clue why that one 20-dollar bill should be so vital. In fact, he couldn't honestly remember having a 20-dollar bill at all at that time.

"The cop then went on to explain, though plainly he believed Bob really knew all the time and was only playing at being innocent. It seems that among the money left in the safe there had been a wad of 20-dollar bills fresh from the bank, all numbered in sequence, so the customer who had paid them in for his purchase could tell the numbers from the ones he had left. The bill in Bob's wallet was from that series.

"Bob was absolutely shattered. He was taken away, charged, and released on bail. He came over to see me that night looking so white and drawn I could hardly recognize his face. Usually, like most people for whom truth is a constant companion, he had an open face, every muscle relaxed. Now he looked aged.

"We talked long and prayed. We read Scripture together. I had no doubts about his innocence, of course, and neither did anyone else in our group once the news got out. They all knew him too well. As we went over and over everything, there was only one scenario that fit the facts, and that was that he had been framed by his manager, a Christian of standing, known to us all. That bill was a plant, and the whole thing was done out of the man's vindictiveness because Bob had stood up to him.

"What could be done? We could try making counter-accusations, but we doubted whether we could make them stick. It was going to be Christian against Christian in the courts anyway, and with only one reputation for honesty being able to survive the combat there seemed little doubt that it would be the older man who would be upheld. *We* knew our Bob to be innocent, but we would be considered partisan.

I must say, Bob's parents were marvelous to him over it all. They believed him innocent, and although they didn't have much time for his Christianity, they did respect his Christian standards. His mom came to see me. 'Honest,' she said, 'he wouldn't be taking an extra spoonful of sugar for his coffee without telling me.'

"As you can guess, the affair absorbed oceans of my time over the next few weeks. A lot of it was in prayer. We were hanging on to that text I mentioned when we were talking about Abigail and Georgina earlier this evening! '"It is mine to avenge; I will repay," says the Lord' (Rom. 12:19) and 'no weapon forged against you will prevail, and you will refute every tongue that accuses you'" (Isa. 54:17).

Mike, greatly impressed by all he'd heard so far of Bob's steadfast integrity, broke in with a question.

"Didn't Bob waver in all this?"

"There was one time when we talked long into the night when he brought out of the dark recesses of his soul the depression and doubts that had been gathering there. He'd been reluctant to admit their existence until then. He told me how he'd been bothered by the devil telling him that the mess he was in was all his own silly fault. If he hadn't been such a stickler for truth, that hypocritical turkey of a manager wouldn't have done this to him. Then again, why wasn't he making life hell for that man if he was so sure he'd framed him? If he threw enough mud at him he'd get some to stick and then at least they would both sink together. The devil even got him to think that maybe becoming a Christian was a mistake in the first place. He should have kept away from all these people who were either weird or hypocrites.

"As is usually the case with that wily old buzzard, there was more than a grain of truth in the devil's arguments. It was quite true that it was only because Bob was so committed to absolute honesty in everything that he had raised the ire of his boss. And it was true that it was his Christian beliefs that had made him so firm in that commitment. And look where it had landed him!"

"So how did you counsel him?" Mike asked.

"Well, I had to point out that this was the way it would often be in this sinful world. I showed him those passages in 1 Peter which talk about suffering unjustly. You know, a lot of those early Christians faced trumped-up charges, and many of them died as a result. Most of all, though, we should never lose sight of the fact that Jesus Himself was framed by false witnesses. If the proper justice for which Rome was famous had been carried out, Jesus would not have been condemned and executed. But He suffered because God had a plan for our salvation. In other words, His suffering was redemptive. Now, of course, there can only ever be one atonement; we can't add anything to the redemption of Christ made on the cross, buying us back from sin and destruction. That's 100 percent complete. Yet at the same time there is a sense in which, when we suffer in His name, our sufferings are also redemptive, part of God's great plan to save the world. They're part of Christ's sufferings. I think Paul was talking along those lines when he told the Colossians in chapter 1, verse 24, 'I fill up in my flesh what is still lacking in regard to Christ's afflictions, for the sake of his body.'

"The fact of the matter is, bad things do sometimes happen to good people. And things are not always righted this side of eternity."

"As they weren't for Uriah," said Mike, remembering the Bible story that lay open on his lap.

"Too true," said Bill. "But I'm sure he has a very special place in heaven right close to the Lord. And I would make a guess right close to David too, God's grace being the miracle it is. I think it's a lovely touch in the Scriptures that he gets a special mention in the family tree of Jesus in Matthew 1:6, even though, strictly speaking, he was not an actual ancestor."

He realized he was getting away from the story of Bob and could see Mike was anxious to know the climax.

"Back to Bob. As the day of the trial drew nearer, we mounted a continuous prayer watch. The community was buzzing with anticipation. It's a sad fact that bad news is much more exciting than good news to most people. Bob himself had gotten past his depression and had settled himself down in a quiet waiting on God which gave him a deep peace, albeit mixed up with a bit of apprehension. You couldn't help feel the tension closing in on the church like a gathering storm cloud, though.

"But then a day before the case came up, Bob phoned me in an ecstasy of excitement. He had just had a call from his lawyer. The case was dropped. Just like that. He didn't know any details at the time, but he promised to come right over as soon as he had everything clear.

"When he came over a few hours later it was as though he was walking on springs. He bounced into this room and gave me a great big hug, joy bubbling out of him like a six-year-old who's been given free admission to Disneyland for life. He flung himself on that bed over there and just gazed up to the ceiling worshiping God, his deliverer.

"Then he told me what had happened. It seems that over

these weeks that crook of a boss of his had been getting more and more convicted over the awful thing he had done. He clearly wasn't such a hypocrite as we had thought. The Holy Spirit did have access to his heart after all. In the end he couldn't go through with his plan and went and confessed it all."

"What happened to him then?" asked Mike.

"I expect you can guess that Bob certainly did not want to press charges. The police did, because obviously he'd been guilty of some very serious things, and the police hate being made fools of. Well, he was charged, but was let off with a fine, which was some kind of miracle. The great thing about Bob is that he was praying for him almost as much as he had prayed for himself. But the guy couldn't stand the pressure and in the end he left town to make a new start someplace else."

"And Bob?" asked Mike.

"You'll have a chance to ask him yourself in time, no doubt," said Bill. "I think he'll tell you the old adage is true—honesty really does pay. But he'll also tell you it costs you your all."

Chapter 9

"You've certainly had some high drama in your time here at Fairmont," said Mike, thinking back over what he had just heard.

"Life's never dull," agreed Bill with a grin. Then he put on a pseudo-serious face. "You're not thinking of chickening out, are you?"

"No way!" Mike replied, with a decisive turn of his head on each syllable. "The more I hear, the more I want to hear. I can't wait to get started."

"You may change your mind after this next potato-head. He is Mr. Big Trouble himself. I've known him the whole 10 years I've been here, and I never have been able to really tame him. He's a fire-eater of a guy, he's outrageous, and sometimes he acts so stupid you'd think his brains must have blown through his ears in the wind, and yet you can't help liking him. At least, I can't. I have a feeling there are some who would just love to wring his neck."

"Bill, you've got me on the edge of my seat. Who is this guy?"

Without replying, Bill pulled himself around in his chair and began tapping at his computer. On to the screen came the story of the young man Bill had started to describe.

"Chip Martin. Age 19. 412 Orange Grove. Tel: 553-1597. Comments: Erratic, wild, energetic. Christian parents. Strong faith, but no apparent close relationship with God. Too free with the girls. Lacks self-discipline. *Sa.*"

"I reckon you must be thinking of Samson," said Mike, observing the code letters.

"Right on," answered Bill. "He looks a bit like Samson must have looked, too. Big, strong, muscular. A bit of a bozo."

"Bozo?" Mike asked quizzically, cocking his head.

"More brawn than brain," Bill explained. "Not that he's unintelligent—he just doesn't use his grey matter as much as he should sometimes, while his beef gets used more than is healthy—to the annoyance of a great many. But like I said before, I can't help liking Chip. There's a child-likeness about him which wins me over to his side even when he's really gone over the top."

Mike pondered over what Bill had said so far and voiced his thoughts.

"I was reading the story of Samson recently, and it struck me if I dare say it, that the Bible doesn't seem to make its mind up about the man, just like you're in two minds about Chip."

Bill laughed.

"I don't think you'd better let our deacons hear you say the Bible can't make its mind up, but I know what you mean. On the one hand he's portrayed as God's chosen deliverer, rescuing Israel from the Philistines; on the other he's breaking every rule in the book."

While Bill was talking, Mike had been looking up Judges 13. When he had arrived at the passage, he studied it for a few minutes, then spoke. "He certainly seems to have been God's man in a very special sense, doesn't he? I mean, according to this his birth was announced by an angel and took place miraculously, for his mother was infertile."

"That's so," said Bill. "And not only that. By divine order he had to become a Nazirite for life, which meant not touching alcohol or even grapes, never coming into contact with a dead body, and keeping his hair uncut. It was a kind of unique separation to the Lord, a bit like a modern monk or nun taking vows of chastity, obedience, and poverty, I suppose."

"None of that fits Chip, though, surely?"

"I doubt it," chuckled Bill. "His mom and dad have never claimed to have had a vision of angels—as far as I know—and Chip, having two older sisters, rules out any idea of his mom's infertility! No, it's more in the basic character that the parallels come over. Seeing as you've got your Bible open there at the right place, let's just have a look at Samson again.

"The thing that strikes me about him is that he is a loser. Although he's one of Israel's judges, you don't find him leading the troops to battle like most of the others. All his exploits are single-handed. Fantastic feats, I agree; but there doesn't really seem to be any deep feeling of belonging to the people of God. In fact, a lot of what he does appears to be out of personal pique, getting his own back on the Philistines. It's a sort of dirty-tricks competition."

Mike argued an objection, "But you can't get away from the fact that the Bible says plainly that God was inspiring him. His strength is because the Spirit of the Lord is in him and we're even told his first quarrel with the Philistines is through God 'seeking an occasion to confront [them].'" Mike showed the fourth verse of chapter 14 to prove the point.

Bill glanced at it, and then said, "Yes, you're right. But that doesn't mean the Lord approves of Samson's messing around like he did. I would say that the whole weird era of Judges is described right at the end of the book in the very last verse: 'In those days Israel had no king; everyone did as he saw fit.' God had a divine purpose to fulfill, and He used Samson according to the man he was and how he fit into the chaotic standards of the bizarre time he lived in."

"Let me see if I understand what you're saying," Mike said, light beginning to dawn on his confusion. "When Samson told his parents he wanted to marry a Philistine wife, that would be against God's law. But the Lord was prompting him to do it because that was the way Samson operated and God was going to turn that to His glory."

"That's about it," replied Bill. "Otherwise I don't see how we can explain all the other horrible things Samson did. It was a question of the Master Craftsman having to use warped materials."

"You can say that again," Mike said. "Samson wasn't even true to his calling as a Nazirite. I mean, of those three things we mentioned earlier that a Nazirite promised, the only one we can be sure he kept was not to cut his hair. I can't imagine he kept away from the booze, and he certainly touched enough corpses in his time, what with the lot he killed with the donkey jawbone and the 30 men he slaughtered for his friends' wedding presents. Hey!"

Mike suddenly stopped his tirade against Samson and went off on another tack. "The more I say about Samson, the more I wonder what you're going to tell me about Chip. He isn't a crackshot with a jawbone by any chance?"

"Naw . . . " Bill assured him with a deep laugh, "he hasn't hurt anyone that I know of—at least, not physically, though he's broken quite a few hearts on the way."

"Broken hearts?" queried Mike.

"Quite a few," Bill affirmed. "The first ones were his parents. When I came to Fairmont, Chip was only nine. His mom and dad were real kind to me, had me over to meals, made me feel at home; they were great in every way. And they were so proud of Chip. They loved all three of their children, but Chip's arriving last and being a boy gave them an extra thrill. They told me that when he had been dedicated in church, they added a prayer of their own that the Lord would take him and use him for whatever task He wanted: missionary, minister, evangelist, just anything as long as he was wholly the Lord's.

"Well, by the time I arrived on the scene he had grown up to be a real harum-scarum. But his parents took it to be the pranks of a normal fun-loving youngster. They'd spank him and correct him with love and tears, but it didn't make a great deal of difference.

"As I watched him in those early years I could see him getting worse rather than better. But when he was 12 he came to his Sunday School teacher and said he wanted to become a Christian. We were all thrilled, of course—especially his parents—and we looked for great changes."

"And were there?" asked Mike.

"Yes and no," Bill answered. "On the one hand, he was quite sure that he had been born again, and wasn't afraid to say so. On the other hand, his life really didn't match up to his profession. In fact, the older he got, the more wild he seemed to become. When he was old enough to get his first motorbike, wow! You should have seen him burn up the road on that thing. You could hear him coming five blocks away, and you took cover. He'd roar past with his handlebars set so high you'd swear he'd need boathooks to hang on to them, and if you were on the road at the same time, watch out. The local chapter of Hell's Angels practically retired to the next town in fright of him. I think we were all relieved when he finally wrapped it around a fire hydrant, though no doubt he'll get another soon. So watch out—check your life insurance.

"More serious, though, is his relationship with the other sex. Girls, girls, girls."

Bill shook his head sorrowfully.

"He'll never learn. The thing is, although he gets them as easy as cracking peanuts, they twist him around their little fingers. They've made a fool of him time and again. And made him poor."

Mike recalled in his mind how Samson got himself into trouble through his female attachments, culminating in Delilah's betrayal of him that cost him his hair, his strength, his eyes, and finally his life. Was Bill, the bachelor, being a bit too eager to link up Chip with Samson?

He put his doubt into words. "Are you saying that just because Chip is something of a rover that he ought not to have girl friends? He's not liable to meet a Delilah, after all, is he?"

Bill leaned back in his chair and spoke slowly.

"Mike, don't ever get the impression from me that I don't like to see boys going out with girls in our group. I think you'll have gathered from my reactions to Joe and Georgina earlier, that's not true. But Chip goes out with girls for all the wrong reasons. He doesn't ever give himself time to have a proper relationship with any depth to it. Apart from that, I'm not so naive as to think he just takes them to the movies and then shakes hands to say goodnight at their front door. The guy is using girls and using sex to satisfy his passing whims."

Without having met Chip or knowing the girls he was dating, Mike knew he was in no position to continue that particular line of conversation.

"Do you think he is really a Christian?" he asked.

"In spite of everything, yes, I do," replied Bill. "Sometimes he can show the most amazing faith, just like Samson did that time when he was thirsty and trusted the Lord for a miraculous supply of water (see Judg. 15:18). And he does believe God has a plan for his life. But his trouble is he is so totally undisciplined."

He paused, trying to piece things together in his mind to form a judgment.

"I think," said Bill at last, "that his main problem is he does not have a deep relationship with the Lord. He knows Him and yet he doesn't *know* Him. As old-fashioned as it sounds, I believe in the absolute necessity of a daily quiet time with the Lord—a period with your Bible and with prayer, preferably in the morning."

"Amen!" Mike heartily assented.

"Now I am fairly confident that Chip has never truly known that. He's been told of course, and he's heard sermons on it no doubt, but he hasn't put it into practice. If he doesn't allow the Word of God to soak into him then it will never become part of him to shape his life and influence all his actions and reactions."

Mike felt himself right on Bill's wavelength at this point.

"I can see now why you are so keen to identify Chip with Samson, because that seems to have been his trouble too. In spite of his great faith in God, and the exploits he did in the Lord's name, you never get the impression he walked with God. We find him praying in emergencies, but we never find him worshiping, do we?"

Bill nodded. "I'm sure you're right. And the lack of communion with the Lord shows itself, I think, in the way that when the Spirit of the Lord left him after Delilah had lopped off his hair, he didn't even realize it."

The point raised another query in Mike's mind.

"Since you mention it, that does bother me a little. First,

how do you account for the Spirit of the Lord using a rascal like Samson, and then having possessed the Spirit, how could he lose Him?"

Bill answered, "I think we have to accept that the Spirit operated differently in the Old Testament to the way He does now with us Christians. Then, the Spirit was given for specific tasks, and often only given temporarily. Sometimes, even non-followers of the Lord were anointed by the Spirit—for example, King Cyrus of Persia. But we Christians are given the Spirit permanently to live within us, and being the *Holy* Spirit, there is the requirement that we are holy too, which means to become more like Jesus."

"Where does that leave our wayward Chip?" Mike wanted to know.

"Well, I don't believe he will be lost to the Lord, for I believe he is saved right through to eternity if he came in true repentance and faith that time. But I do believe that he will suffer some sort of eternal loss if there is no fruit of righteousness in his life. Don't ask me exactly how that will work out in heaven, because I don't know. God hasn't told us. But He has told us enough to be sure that Christians cannot sin with impunity. We must all appear before the judgment seat of Christ."

"'Saved, but only as one escaping through the flames'—1 Corinthians 3:15," quoted Mike from memory.

"That's right," said Bill, "but my prayer is that long before that happens, Chip will get his life in order, stop his erratic behavior, and really find out what God wants him to do with his life. Samson left it much too late before he prayed the first prayer he ever prayed. Let's ask the Lord to bring Chip to full surrender soon. How about a prayer time now before you go home?"

Chapter 10

The next night, it was lightly raining as Mike made his way to Bill's apartment, and the deserted Fairmont streets had a forlorn greyness about them. The effect on Mike was to induce in him a slight apprehension as he thought of the years ahead. Would he make it? Would he be accepted by the people here, especially the young people themselves? How would they receive the gospel from him with his weird English accent? If only you could buy experience as a ready-mix instead of having to earn it the long, painful way.

His preoccupation almost made him walk right past the apartment house. As it was, he went a few yards past the entrance before bringing himself back to this planet and this time, and he spun quickly around on the sidewalk with a self-rebuking grunt, almost embarrassed at his mistake, though there was no one around to observe it. He gave a sharp double prod on the button next to the name tab "Pulkington" and after a cheery greeting from Bill through the speaker-grille, there was a protracted click indicating that the electronic lock had worked and the door was now free—a fact confirmed as it yielded to Mike's tentative push.

A short ride in the elevator brought Mike to Bill's door, already open in welcome. As Mike stepped in he had something of a shock. Last night he had left a room as tangled as a plate of spaghetti. Now he found himself in a room as straight and orderly as a box of new pencils.

Bill was obviously anticipating Mike's surprise. He stood there, his legs casually astride, hands resting lightly in the pockets of his jeans, that craggy face of his wrinkled in amused delight.

Mike gave a long "Whewww" of a whistle. "My word, you *have* been working hard," he said.

"Oh, I can do it when I put my mind to it," the pastor replied with an airy off-handedness.

"Don't you believe a word of it!" came a female voice from around the corner of the alcove where Bill's computer was housed. The voice gave Mike yet another surprise. He hadn't realized anyone else was there.

The owner of the voice came out from the alcove, followed by Joe, both grinning broadly.

Bill sighed with pretended disappointment.

"OK, I suppose I'd better come clean. This," he said, waving his hand to the attractive red-head, "in case you haven't guessed it, is Georgina. I've just been helping her with a little problem."

Georgina exploded with indignation as phony as Bill's disappointment.

"What he means is, I've been here most of the day, slaving like a convict on hard labor, getting him packed and ready to go, which is only to be expected since we can't wait to get rid of him."

Now the sham attitudes couldn't be maintained any longer. For with that last statement Georgina's eyes filled up. She obviously cared very, very much that this man who had seen her through so many crises was about to leave. It made Mike feel even more in trepidation about taking over.

The artificial atmosphere was pierced by Joe.

"Well, what are we all waiting for? Let' sit down and relax. I'm dying for some coffee"—though from the way he was eyeing the tin by the side of the coffee machine it was obvious his desires were more on Georgina's cookies than what he would be washing them down with.

With the apartment at last in a neat and tidy state they were all able, for once, to find something to sit on designed for the purpose, though Joe and Georgina seemed to prefer to share a bean bag and leave the offered chairs vacant.

As they drank, ate, and chatted, Mike decided to voice something of his misgivings.

"Bill," he began, "I think over these last couple of nights you've been doing something really tremendous. You've let me into some important insights about folk I'll be involved with and you've shown me how it all links up with the Bible. It's been great. But the trouble is, Bill, it's left me just plain scared. I'm not sure I can cope—or perhaps I should say I'm more and more sure I can't cope."

"Ah, my son Timothy," Bill said with solemn good humor, "God hasn't given you a spirit of fear—remember?"

"That's all very well," persisted Mike, who remembered very clearly the first night and their discussion of Paul's hesitant aide-de-camp, "but I've got to face facts, and having seen your gifts and what you've achieved I'm wondering if I'm in the right job."

"But we haven't been talking just about the winners, have we? I've shared with you some of the failures too. There are times when I feel I've made a mess of things, but I know I've got to keep my eye on the Lord, be faithful, and leave the results to Him."

Joe cut in on the conversation.

"Bill, I remember you doing a Bible study with me once in one of our staff meetings, where you explained how you felt a particular period in Paul's ministry was a kind of model for the way your work here panned out."

"Paul at Athens, you mean? Yes, that's right."

"Why not explain it again? I think it would help Mike," Joe suggested.

"Alright, why not? We can leave the computer for a bit. Let's all get our Bibles."

The four fetched their Scriptures and sat down.

"Acts 17:16," pronounced Bill, though his three companions were already well on the way to locating the passage.

"Let's read a few verses each," Bill suggested, a suggestion which was immediately taken up with an "OK, I'll start," from Joe.

As Georgina, the last of the four to read, finished off the chapter, eyes were fixed on Bill waiting for him to begin. He, however, was looking at Mike.

"Tell me, how does Fairmont strike you as a town?" he asked him.

Mike was uncertain what sort of answer Bill was looking for. Should he show a warm appreciation of the place, and make vague "wonderful-to-be-here"-type statements?

He decided to be as honest as possible. "I like it, but it's not like home," he said briefly.

"That's not quite what I meant. Spiritually, what do you think of it?"

"I don't think I can really say yet," replied Mike. "I see a lot of churches, and the one Sunday I was here they all seemed fairly well-attended, but that's no indication of spiritual life, I know."

"That's right!" Bill agreed. "I asked because I believe one of the first things you need to do when you arrive in a town to begin ministry there is assess what sort of a place it is. That's what Paul did when he came to Athens, and I followed his example."

"And what did you think of us all those years ago?" Georgina asked, a twinkle in her eye and with particular interest as a lifelong Fairmonter.

"It was amazingly close to Paul's estimate of Athens. Oh, I don't mean intellectually—you're all a bunch of blue-grass hillbillies here." Gentle teasing was never far away when Bill was talking.

"But you don't have to be a Stoic or Epicurean or any other of those philosophy nuts that Paul found swarming around Athens to have the same basic problem that city had."

"Which was what?" asked Mike.

"Why, what it says right here in verse 16—the place was full of idols. Their idols would be carved figures of one sort or another; you don't see too many of those around in Fairmont. But idols there are in plenty. When I saw the way this American town was so self-satisfied, with people concerned for their big salaries, their nice homes, their comfortable life-style, their status in business or in the community, I thought to myself, 'Boy, these people are idolaters; they're worshiping *themselves*. God isn't in their lives at all, even if they do go to church!' And like Paul got upset at Athens, I got upset at Fairmont."

"But how about the church?" Mike interjected. "Surely that was a big positive plus."

"Not really," said Bill, resuming his melancholy account. "You may recall when I told you about Abe and Cindy, that things were somewhat wobbly here in those days, partly because of their leadership—or lack of it. The group then was suffering from a severe case of Athens disease."

"Alright, tell us—what's that?" Georgina asked with a puzzled smile.

"Oracle-itis, which is inflammation of the know-all gland. Symptoms: certain you know the truth; a compulsion to say so; a craving to argue with anyone who disagrees. Ten years ago was just about the time all those weird cults were spreading like a rash—you may remember, no, it's only me who's that ancient. Anyway, that was when people were going overboard for Eastern mysticism, odd-all pseudo-Christian communes, drug experiments, and lots more. Just like those philosophy freaks in Athens that the Bible tells us 'spent their time doing nothing but talking about and listening to the latest ideas.' Uh . . . verse 21," he added, remembering this was supposed to be a Bible study.

"So," he went on, "putting together the smug status quo of the town as a whole, and the mess of confused thinking of the kids I was supposed to be pastoring, and I reckoned I had my Athens. Now the problem was, how do I crack the nut? What was the way to begin to win these people for the Lord? What would you have done, Mike, if you had come on the scene when I came?"

Mike was beginning to get used to Bill's disconcerting questions which prevented anyone from ever being a mere passive listener. He made a mental note to build the same habit into his Bible study technique. He tried to formulate an answer to the question.

"Prayer, first of all," he answered. "But I guess you want me to say more than that."

Bill's nod showed he did, so Mike continued.

"I think as far as the young people were concerned, I'd try to get to know them first, and then argue as patiently as I could with them, pointing them to Christ. As for the *town*, that would have to wait a bit, I think, until I'd gotten a good base to work from in the church."

"Well done!" said Bill encouragingly. "That's almost what I did, but I tied it up much more closely with the passage in Acts we've been reading. I made that my model. Let's look again at what it says."

All four of them let their eyes roam down the 19 verses of Scripture. Bill then directed them to Paul's method.

"You'll notice he spoke both in the synagogue and in the marketplace. It would be stupid to try and make twentieth-century Fairmont an exact copy of first-century Athens, and of course I can't by any stretch of the imagination make 'synagogue' equal 'church.' But all the same, I took that to show me that I ought to get out with the gospel into the community from the word go. I didn't accept the idea 'Let's get the church right first, then we'll evangelize.' So I didn't quite do what you suggested, Mike. The danger of waiting is that tomorrow never comes. I'm not saying there isn't ever a time when you've got to concentrate all your energies on putting your own house in order first, but on the other hand, part of putting any church in order is teaching it its evangelistic priorities. Christ's commission to go and tell is always in force. It's a standing order."

Joe jumped in while Bill paused for breath.

"Apart from that, if Christ really thrills your heart and if you believe without Him people are lost, you can't help but tell others about Him." He began to look a bit crestfallen. "In fact, that's where I've fallen down so often." He tapped his left breast with his open hand. "I just don't feel like I should in here."

Bill said, "I guess none of us is where we should be, as far as that goes. But you're quite right about not being able to keep quiet when we are filled with the Lord. And that's how it was when I began at Fairmont. I looked for every opportunity that I could. I wasn't always wise about it, mind you." He grinned at a sudden memory.

"I did some door-to-door witnessing and I found a great deal of resistance because people thought I was a Jehovah's Witness. So when I came to one door and a lady said, before I could open my mouth, 'Are you a Jehovah's Witness?' looking at me with more suspicion than a Kojak, I quickly replied, 'Indeed, Ma'am, I am *not*!' Then a voice, presumably her husband's, came from inside the house, 'Is that a Jehovah's Witness?' so I said again, 'I can assure you absolutely, *I am not a Jehovah's Witness.*' The lady said with fire in her eyes, 'Well, we are.' It's not often I'm wrong-footed in a conversation, but that certainly was one time!

"Let's get back to Paul at Athens. Fortunately he didn't have Jehovah's Witnesses to cope with, but there were plenty of weird, kooky beliefs. Ironically, it was he who was considered to have the kooky belief."

"If you went to a town where everyone had green spots and you didn't, you'd stand out, wouldn't you?" said Georgina.

"Thanks for that illustration, Georgina," Bill said. "I may use it one day—especially if I ever come across a green-spotted audience.

"However, back in Athens we find Paul being called to give account of himself to the Areopagus. That was a kind of city council. It was very ancient, older than any history book could say. It used to meet on Mars Hill, which is what the word *Areopagus* means, but by Paul's day, though the name had stuck, it met in Athens's marketplace. The council had lost a lot of its old powers but was still responsible for investigating religious and moral affairs."

"Your escapade with the Jehovah's Witnesses didn't get you hauled before the city council, did it?" asked Mike.

"Hardly," chuckled Bill. "I think at that time the council was so apathetic about religious affairs I could have done cartwheels down the street in a saffron robe and it wouldn't have taken any notice. No, what makes Paul's appearance before the Areopagus relevant to me and Fairmont is his tactic.

"I remember, Mike, that you said if you had come to the confused group I came to, you would have argued with them patiently. That's fine—but how would you have argued? What would have been your line?"

Mike knew the answer would be somewhere in this passage of Acts, so he studied it again. As he looked up, he said, "It looks to me as though what Paul tried to do was find common ground. I'm thinking of the way he quotes from their own poets and so on."

Bill looked pleased. His pupil was learning fast! "You're right, of course. But I'm going to press you just a stage further. What do you make of his reference to the altar inscription, 'To an unknown God'?"

"It was a good point of contact, I suppose," answered Mike. "What we were told in sermon class at Bible college was: get a good point of contact, 'cause if you've lost 'em in the first 10 seconds, you've lost em! But I guess that's not the answer you're looking for. I'm not sure what else."

Georgina intervened. "Could it be that Paul had found the cleft in their armor? I mean, here they were with all their philosophies and religions, idols and shrines, dotted about like mailboxes, and yet this one inscription showed they still weren't absolutely sure they had found *the* answer."

"Absolutely right! Georgina, you're a marvel. All this and cookies too! Great! Yes, I'm sure that is what Paul was doing. He was showing them what the honest Athenians knew deep down in their hearts. For all their gods, they still had a 'God-shaped blank.'

"And that's what I tried to show that original youth group with all their strange ideas. It was very demanding on me, because I knew they would be looking at me: how real was Christ in my own life? Was I living in the power of Jesus myself by His Spirit? One of the things that strikes me about Paul's letters is the way that when his authority is being challenged he invites his readers to look at his life and ministry and judge him on the strength of that. That's a mighty risky thing to do unless you're delivering the goods with no short weight.

"So I endeavored to demonstrate to the youth group what they were missing. In what I said and what I did I wanted them to see 'The Unknown God,' and then not just to know about Him but to truly know Him in all His love, holiness, and power. But I knew I had to meet them on their ground, just like Paul did the Athenians. Do you realize when he talked with them, he didn't quote the Bible once, but he did quote pagan poets with approval. That was really becoming all things to all men."

Mike interrupted. "Just a minute though, Bill. We had one lecturer at Bible college who reckoned Paul was such a flop at Athens using his get-on-their-level approach that he abandoned the method ever after. He quoted what Paul wrote to Corinth, which of course was the next place he visited. He told them 'I resolved to know nothing while I was with you except Jesus Christ and him crucified (1 Cor. 2:2).' What is your answer to that?"

"I disagree wholly," replied Bill. "Apart from anything else, I would deny that Paul's visit to Athens was a flop, as we shall see in a moment. There are other reasons why I disagree, which I'll go into some other time, but meanwhile let's remember it was to the Corinthians themselves that Paul described his strategy like this: 'To those under the law I became like one under the law . . . so as to win those under the law. To those not having the law I became like one not having the law, . . . so as to win those not having the law. To the weak I became weak, to win the weak. I have become all things to all men so that by all possible means I might save some' (1 Cor. 9:20-22).

"Well, for better or for worse—I'm sure it was for better. That's the policy I adopted here at Fairmont. I got to know what they believed—what was good about it, what was wrong with it. I commended what I could commend and opposed what I had to oppose, all the while loving them as much as the Lord put love in my heart to love them with.

"But I learned something that I should have been ready for from the very model I was using here in Acts 17. And that was that however much you are trying to identify with the folk you want to win, sooner or later there will come a crunch point of disagreement.

"Perhaps I can best illustrate it by telling you about Joan Berkhof. You remember Joan?" Bill asked Joe and Georgina, who both nodded.

"Joan was a super girl. She was one of those who could always be relied on in a crisis. If you went on a youth picnic and found you'd forgotten the buns, she'd be the one who would pedal off to the store on her bike and come back balancing a hundred on her handlebars.

"Well, Joan was an 'almost' Christian. She accepted practically everything, and a lot of her questions I'd answer and she'd say, 'Yes, I see that now.' I had tremendous hope for her, and never doubted that one day she'd come all the way.

"Well, you can imagine what a thrill it was when one night—it was at the end of a barbecue as it happened, and yes, I do believe it was the one when she'd cycled off to get the buns. Where was I?—oh, yes, Joan came to me and said she'd like to accept the Lord as her Saviour. So we sat down together, she and I, on a little clump of grass in the sand dune and I pulled out my New Testament and a little gospel booklet. I told her God loved her and had a plan for her life, and she nodded. Then I showed her how sin had made a gulf between her and God, and that must mean eternal separation and death. I noticed she wasn't nodding this time. 'I know I sin, and I know that grieves God, but I can't believe He would condemn me for it. I believe He forgives us all, whether we accept Christ or not.'

"I guess a lot of people believe that," I said, "but let's see what the Bible says" and I showed her various texts—Romans 3:23, Romans 6:23, and so on. But all to no avail. In the end we had to leave it, and what had begun so promisingly ended so unhappily for us both. As far as I know, she has never gotten beyond that point, though I must admit I've lost touch with her now.

"That was her sticking point. With Paul at Athens, it was the Resurrection. Those Greeks simply could not believe in something so grossly physical as resurrection. It wasn't refined. It didn't fit the way they believed things should be done. For all his willingness to adapt, Paul could not compromise on that point. So that had to be that."

"Then it was a flop, wasn't it?" questioned Joe. "There were only a few converted."

"Only a few! In Athens! Call that a flop?"

Joe had touched Bill on a nerve.

Bill swept on, "It was the most amazing miracle that *anyone* was converted. When I think how long it took for me to see any fruit here in Fairmont when I had so much more in my favor than Paul did, I have nothing but holy envy for what happened there. You can be sure if the Acts of the Apostles mentions somebody by name, it means they became well-known, so that people reading the book would recognize them and say, 'Oh, so that's where old so-and-so comes into it.' I reckon Dionysius and Damaris were in that category, truly significant Christians, and of course they weren't the only converts. No, I reckon it was a significant gospel victory that day in Athens.

"I will grant you this, though. Paul being the big-hearted evangelist he was, I'm sure he must have gone to his lodgings that night crying bitter tears that so many had rejected the Lord. And that will be your heartbreak too, Mike, here in Fairmont, as it's been mine. Why anyone should reject such a gracious offer is beyond comprehension, but the sad fact is they do. Still, cheer up. It's all worth it. How do you feel about things now, Mike?"

"I still think it's pretty daunting. But you've given me a plan of campaign that seems practical. I've also learned not to be afraid of failure."

"That's right," said Bill. "And believe me, God will give you your Dionysius and your Damaris even when it feels like almost everyone is laughing in your face.

"But now let's get to the computer. I've got a real winner to cheer us all up. C'mon and see."

Chapter 11

To arrange chairs for four in the tiny alcove involved a lot of shuffling around, but eventually Mike, Joe, and Georgina were all able to get an unimpeded view of the screen with Bill in control, sitting in front on his swivel chair.

He hadn't told Joe and Georgina who he had in mind to talk about next, so when the name Laura Hermanez appeared it was as much a revelation to them as it was to Mike. Two simultaneous whoops of delight from them both told Mike that Laura was a Number One hit.

Bill was transparently pleased at the reaction of his two young people. "Here she is, everybody's sweetheart. Mike, you're going to love this. Here's a winner if ever there was one—someone who can teach us all something."

"Right on . . . " said Joe enthusiastically. "Laura's the girl to boost anybody's faith. I really go for her."

Georgina did not seem the slightest bit put out by this apparent announcement of a rival for the affections of her fiancé. She knew what he meant, and she was as fond of Laura as Joe was. In fact, she counted her as a special friend whose love and vibrant trust in the Lord had meant a lot to her during her years of trial with her father.

All this vigorous warmth towards Laura made Mike study

the screen with keenness in order to see what it was that so commended the young lady to his friends. He read:

"Laura Hermanez: Age 19. Address: 1839 East 43rd Street. Tel: 555-1680. Comments: Half-Mexican. Non-Christian parents. Fiery nature, aggressive faith, very determined, winsome. *SP.*"

Mike was a little puzzled.

"I don't quite understand," he said. "From the way you all reacted I thought I was going to read about a pleasant, quiet, girl. Instead of that, your comments up there, Bill, speak to me of a bit of a wildcat. Frankly, I'm a bit scared of meeting her, if that's an accurate picture."

The three friends almost fell off their seats laughing. Georgina was the first to subside enough to get some words out in reply, though even then with difficulty.

"S-s-s-sorry, Mike," she stuttered, "but the thought of Laura, the Latin-American wildcat scratching your eyes out is just too much. Wait till I tell her. She's not like that at all—well, at least, not unless roused." Georgina's eyes sparkled with good humor.

"Don't forget the last word of the comments," prompted Joe, leaning forward to underline "winsome" with his finger.

"That's something else I don't quite understand," Mike replied, looking not at all happy at his treatment. "That word doesn't seem to fit the rest."

"Does the biblical code help you at all?" Bill inquired.

"*SP*—um, not much," said Mike. "The only Bible character I can think of with those initials is Simon Peter. And it can't be him, can it?"

"No, it's not," Bill confirmed. "To be honest, it's a little bit of a cheat, because *SP* doesn't stand for the name of a person at all, but a place. That's not to trip you up, but only because this particular character is anonymous in the Bible."

"Can't guess. You tell me." Mike was getting a bit tired of being kept on a string.

"Alright—Syro-Phoenicia. Does it click?"

The clouds cleared from Mike's face. "Of course," he said. "Now don't tell me—Matthew 15:21 and Mark 7:24?"

"That's another gold star on your merit card," Bill congratulated him. "You know your Bible well."

"I preached on that passage a fortnight ago," Mike confessed, "so it's still fresh in my mind."

"In that case," said Bill, "you'd be able to tell me more about this lady than I can tell you, and you can judge for yourself if I'm right to link her up with our delightful Laura. Let's all turn to the passage, folks, before we go any further."

To find Matthew presented little problem to four regular readers of the Good Book, and in seconds they were all ready.

"Right," said Bill. "Seeing as you've read the passage more recently than the rest of us, Mike, you give us a brief run-down on it, and tell us what you think about this unknown lady."

He wagged his finger at Mike. "But no preaching your sermon to us, mind you!"

Mike drew a deep breath and prepared to launch into his analysis of one of his favorite Bible passages. Georgina and Joe, hands held, smiled encouragingly.

"The way it looks to me," Mike started, "this is all about not taking no for an answer, even from God. You see, I don't think Jesus ever would refuse anyone who came to Him. After all, He said Himself, 'Whoever comes to me I will never drive away,' so all that Jesus was doing when He told the Syro-Phoenician woman that He was only sent to the lost sheep of Israel was testing her faith. Her faith passed the test with her clever reply about the dogs picking up the crumbs from under the table, so He met her request and her daughter was healed. There! How did I do?"

"Fine, just fine," Bill answered him, spreading his hand in a gesture of approval. "But let's probe down just a little deeper. And I do have just one small area of disagreement."

Mike lifted his eyebrows and pushed his bottom lip up into the upper one in a look of surprise.

"I think that Jesus at this time *was* only sent to the lost sheep of Israel. You might recall how in the last week of His life Andrew and Philip brought some Greeks to see Jesus, and Jesus didn't see them, but instead gave that little picture of what His death would be like."

"You mean the seed falling into the ground and bringing a great harvest?" Joe asked.

"That's right. I think that shows that worldwide salvation was not going to be poured out from its Jewish container until after the Resurrection. So Jesus wasn't playing with that lady from Syro-Phoenicia—or Canaan, as Matthew calls it. Officially, there was no salvation for Gentiles at that time."

"That's another good sermon spoiled," said Mike, gloomily.

"Not at all," rejoined Bill across a mimed violin duet of "Hearts and Flowers" from Georgina and Joe.

"Actually," he went on, "I think you'll find that you've got a better sermon now, because I believe realizing that Jesus wasn't just teasing or even testing her but stating the actual truth in a gentle way makes the power of her faith even more vivid. You come to see that it is 100 percent true that nothing is impossible to the one who believes."

Joe decided it was time he fed something into the discussion.

"I remember reading a book by a Bible teacher called Derek Prince. He said something like 'We do not question the reality of what our senses reveal, but we do question its finality.'"

Mike nodded his agreement vigorously.

"That sums up exactly what I'm trying to say, and it described perfectly the lady in our Bible story. She knew what Jesus said was true, but she also knew from all she had seen and heard that Jesus was absolute goodness and love. So her faith in Him gave her the confidence to turn His own metaphor against Him. If it's not irreverent to say so, even though it was the Lord she was speaking to, she had the last word. And He was delighted that she did."

"You still haven't told me about your Mexican wildcat," Mike reminded Bill.

"True enough. OK, where shall I start? Her background, as it says on the computer, is half-Mexican. What I haven't got is that she's illegitimate. Her father was in the U.S. Navy and her mother is one of the girls he had in every port, as you might say. After Laura was born, her mom brought her across the border illegally into the States. She says she was looking for the father—whether that's true or not I don't know. In any event, she wandered around for quite a bit keeping one step ahead of deportation. It was really tough for her and Laura in those days.

"Eventually, the legal position got kinda sorted out by her marrying a U.S. citizen—if you saw the Metropolitan Garage on the way into town, that's his. Uh, he's the service attendant, not the manager. It's not a brilliant marriage, but it holds together—just.

"Laura was about 13 at the time, and as soon as she got set up in her new home, she started coming to our church. It was a bit of a new experience for her. Her mother was an umpteenth-generation Catholic who hardly ever went. Her beliefs were weird and much as I disagree about so much with my good friend Father Flanagan who lives across the street, I wouldn't do the injustice to him of saying her weird superstitions were his fault or his church's. Still, it meant that Laura had a lot to unlearn before she could see straight to know what the gospel was, and as we ourselves were only just pulling clear of the mess of the Abe and Cindy era, it meant it was quite a while before Laura got a firm hold on faith in Jesus alone.

"For example, for ages she would wander round with a Saint Christopher medal around her neck, and she had a habit of crossing herself and genuflecting every time she came into our church."

"I remember that," said Joe, laughing. "We used to rib her about it a lot, all in good fun."

Bill was not laughing as he replied. "Joe, I know you well enough to know that you meant no harm. But I can tell you from my pastor's eye view that was not true of the group as a whole. There was malice in a lot of the teasing. And I'm ashamed to say it of a Christian organization, a lot of that malice was born out of prejudice."

"Prejudice?" asked Joe indignantly, feeling ashamed that his senior partner should have found the teasing of which he had been part so objectionable. "How come?"

"I would say because of three things. Her birth, her race, her religious background."

"Oh, come off it, Bill!" Joe exploded, stung by what he wrongly felt was a personal accusation.

Mike looked from one to the other. He had never seen the mild-mannered assistant so agitated.

Bill's laughter lines for once were regimented into a serious frown. "I mean it, Joe," he said, looking him directly in the eye. "I know you were innocent. Bless you, there's not an ounce of guile in you, and I mean that. But you didn't have the discernment to see you were being sucked into a very nasty mutilation of a girl's character and dignity."

Joe was silent. He had been so looking forward to this particular file, and it had gone sour on him.

Bill sighed. "I'm afraid it's something that happens all the time wherever people meet as a group, even when they're Christians. As far as Laura was concerned, what made it worse for her was that these were her years of adolescence, with all those feminine hormonal changes that we mere males know so little about and never understand. So an already fiery temperament had to cope with all kinds of emotional stress, and in the nature of things the more she blew up and threw a tantrum the more she got ridiculed."

"But it was about that time she became a Christian, wasn't it?" Georgina asked.

"That's right," replied Bill. "And you, Joe, had a lot to do with it."

Joe brightened considerably at this information, which was as much news to him as had been his pastor's views on his teasing of Laura. For the second time in the conversation he asked, "How come?" this time with a happier tone to his voice.

"It was as a result of a talk you gave in the youth den one night. She didn't say anything to you then; in fact, it wasn't till long after that she told me, but that night she went home, knelt by her bed, and prayed the sinner's prayer. She thanked the Lord for loving her and dying for her; she asked Him to forgive her sins and to take over her life.

"Do you know what the passage was you based your message on?"

Joe shrugged, "How can I after all this time? Give us a clue."

"Let me guess," burst in Georgina. "The Syro-Phoenician woman."

"You've got it," said Bill. "It spoke to her more powerfully than anything she ever heard before. She told me how she'd been impressed by the way you'd stressed in your message that the Syro-Phoenician woman was an outsider. The disciples wanted to send her away as a nuisance. Even Jesus seemed to say she didn't belong. And that was just how she felt. All that teasing had made her feel horribly isolated, and the fact that she had to get used to having a new stepfather around the house after having her mother to herself all her life had made matters worse.

"Joe, your message must have come straight from heaven that night, because she saw that whatever anybody else said didn't matter. If she came to Jesus in faith, He would accept her, no matter what. She told me that after she prayed it was as though her whole room filled with light. She jumped up and spent the next hour dancing, laughing, and singing."

Joe was visibly moved by all he had heard. To hear of someone accepting Christ's offer of salvation through a message he had given thrilled him to the depths of his soul. Far from this session going sour on him, he now realized it had brought him more joy than he ever imagined possible. He squeezed Georgina's hand in delight. She was overjoyed herself, partly on his behalf but also because it explained to her why Laura had such an inspiring effect on others now. Someone who had learned the power of faith against the odds like that was obviously going to be the most effective encourager of others.

Meanwhile, Mike was also considerably cheered. Having identified so closely with Joe over these last two nights, sharing as they did Timothy's characteristics, he saw how God could use the diffident and shy, even when they did not realize it. All those years ago the Lord had spoken through Joe to Laura and he had not been aware of it. "Cast your bread upon the waters, for after many days you will find it again," he thought to himself, quoting Ecclesiastes 11:1.

Bill was tapping the sides of his computer with a galloping motion of his fingers, thinking deeply.

"I've had another thought about Laura. Talking about her tonight and having gone through the other files so recently, I can see a link with two of the other women and their biblical doubles we've discussed. I'm leaving you out, Georgina—I don't want to embarrass you.

"First, there's Mary and Pat. Remember how I identified them with passive, accepting faith? I seem to recall I said then that that wasn't the only kind of faith. There was the aggressive sort as well, and the two belong together. Well, here it is. This Syro-Phoenician woman provides the perfect complement to Mary as far as faith is concerned."

"That's a really good point," said Mike, responding to the extra insight. "Though come to think of it, Mary herself wasn't entirely devoid of faith that won't take no for an answer, was she?"

"You're thinking of the wedding feast at Cana?" Georgina asked.

"Yes, that's right," Mike replied. "Like the Syro-Phoenician, Mary seemed to have been rebuffed by Jesus, but she didn't give in. She simply told the attendants to carry on and follow her Son's instructions."

Bill followed on. "As we said that first night, a true faith embraces both kinds—the sort that accepts what God sends and the sort that challenges apparently insurmountable obstacles. I think one of the most difficult things in the Christian life is knowing which sort is right at a particular time. Take healing, for example. When do I say I am not going to be healed, so may the Lord help me to bear this affliction? And when do I say this illness is not of the Lord—I believe He wants me to trust Him for complete recovery, however impossible it seems medically?"

The other three waited for the answer but were disappointed, for Bill continued.

"There is no easy way to know. Each case is unique. We have to learn to listen closely to what God is saying. On the one hand, we mustn't tell Him what to do and use faith as a kind of puppet string to manipulate Him to dance to our tune. But on the other hand, we can too easily use the prayer 'your will be done' in the wrong way, as an excuse to never put our faith on the line and trust Him for a miracle." Bill paused thoughtfully for a moment, and then added: "You know, I think that sometimes

God uses extremist healing groups to shame us for our spineless approach to miracles—not that I agree with those who believe it's always God's will to heal."

As so often when the subject of healing is raised, it looked as though the conversation was going to get absorbed on the one subject, so Bill abruptly changed direction to get back to his comparison between the women on his computer file.

"Coming back to our friend Laura. The other contrast I would draw is a totally different one. It's with Cindy, our late, lamented version of Jezebel."

The others were clearly taken aback at this unlikely parallel.

Bill explained further. "They do share a number of things in common. Both vivacious, both exhibiting a determination that's hard to resist. Then both had strange, unbiblical views mixed up with superstition; again, both had their disappointments. But what a difference in the way they handled those things! Cindy pursued her own selfish desires to what, for her, was literally the bitter end. She used her determination in a thoroughly negative way and she took her disappointments as reason for going further and further from God. Laura, on the other hand, turned her determination into an armored car to drive her faith through all the bombshells of disappointment to win right through to the Lord.

"It proves the point I've been making all along: we all have the potential for being winners. It's no good blaming our circumstances if we end up losers. Others have faced the same things and finished up on the victory side."

Mike expressed his agreement. "What you're saying, Bill, is that it's not what happens to us that determines our destiny so much as what we do with what happens."

"That's right," said Bill. "And I'd be more than happy to feel that I've responded as positively to all my disappointments as Laura did to hers."

"And still does," said Georgina with feeling.

"And still does," agreed Bill.

Chapter 12

The happy ending to Laura's story put them all in high spirits. No one wanted to rush on to the next computer file immediately. Bill, Joe, and Georgina got up from their chairs and walked into the main living area of the apartment, joking and bantering with each other.

Mike stood between Bill's swivel chair and computer desk, studying the machine, something he hadn't had much of a chance to do up to now. His earlier impressions of a magnificent machine were confirmed. He knew a little about the subject because he had had a small home model himself, but this was something that would not be out of place in a sizable office.

He stood there admiring it for a couple of minutes, afraid to touch it lest he lose Bill's loaded youth file program. He was wondering what games Bill might have stored in his floppy collection, when an idea surfaced suddenly in his mind.

He turned and called out to the three buddies. "Hey, something just struck me!"

They all looked over to the alcove. Bill said, "You sound like Christopher Columbus making landfall. What've you found?"

"I haven't found anything," Mike responded. "But it just occurred to me that Bill's got all the youth group filed on this computer of his. Right?"

"Right," three voices chimed back.

"And yet there's one important name missing—his own."

"Wow! What an omission!" Bill said in exaggerated irony. "Now I shall never be famous. Still, I'll do my best to remember who I am until modern technology catches up with even me."

Mike was not put off and pursued his Great Idea. He waved a forefinger in the general direction of Joe and Georgina.

"Why don't we three compose a file on Bill right now? Let's turn the tables on him."

Mike's brainwave sparked immediate enthusiasm in the two young people.

"Great, super, let's do it," Georgina bubbled, while Joe rubbed his hands in glee.

"Now you're in for it, Pulkington," he threatened. "You squirm while I reveal all your guilty secrets."

One of the essentials of any youth leader is the willingness to be game for anything, and Bill had never been one to chicken out. So his corrugated features wrinkled into his customary grin as he said, "Why not? But I'd better come and show you how to add a file before you crash my whole program. Then you *will* find out the dark side of my character."

He moved over towards the alcove and all four grouped themselves around the computer while Bill called back the main menu, selected "add file," and then stood back.

"There," he said. "Who's going to punch the buttons?"

"Let Mike," Georgina suggested. "It was his idea."

Mike was more than happy to get his hands onto the superb keyboard, and he slid readily onto Bill's swivel chair.

He began by typing Bill's name, then paused. "Age?" he demanded.

Bill covered his mouth with his hand and mumbled into it with deliberate incoherence.

"Say 35," said Georgina. "And I reckon that's giving him the benefit of quite a few years."

For the address, Mike tapped in simply "Here," then added "till Tuesday." A touch of the return key automatically brought up the underlined word "Comment," and at that point he stopped.

"OK, you two, you've known him longer than me. What shall we put?"

Joe winked. "How about 'old, fat, and worn out'?"

Bill cuffed him and retorted, "He means 'mature, well-built, and experienced.'"

Mike chose the second version and waited again.

Bill was more serious now, for he was beginning to feel that, far from being a joke, this could be a very useful exercise perhaps for his young successor, and certainly of benefit to himself. To know what others think of you can, on occasion, help you to maturity. So he made a suggestion.

"Why don't you three get on with it for a while on your own? I'll take a walk around the block and then I'll come back and see where I agree and disagree with your assessment."

Bill's proposal came as a surprise to the other three, who were still treating the whole thing as a giggle—a bit of lighthearted relief. Therefore they argued about it for a few minutes, but in the end the older man's insistence prevailed. So Bill pulled on an extra sweater, gave them a cheery wave, and disappeared through the door.

Bill's transformation of the event into something more serious than they'd intended made the three ponder awhile before starting on their task. As they did so, their original enthusiasm began to wax warm again. Joe and Georgina looked forward to a discussion of a man they greatly loved and admired, while Mike, though he had only become acquainted with Bill recently, was already firmly in the fan club.

Mike waited, hands poised above the keyboard like a motel organist waiting for diners' requests. "What would you say is Bill's most outstanding characteristic?" he asked.

"Humor," said Joe.

"Understanding," Georgina followed, a fraction of a second behind. Then Joe had second thoughts.

"No, humor is an important part of Bill, but it's not the main thing. And anyway, it isn't a specifically Christian quality. I think the fuel core that keeps all the rest of him going is faith."

Georgina vigorously bobbed her red hair up and down, willingly conceding the point.

Mike listed the three qualities on the screen, giving pride of place to faith, and then added the word that was burning at the back of his own mind: perseverance.

"I'm just thinking of all he's been telling me these last couple of nights," he explained. "Bill hasn't had an easy time and he's had to deal with some hairy situations, but he's kept going. He's no quitter. He's built up this youth group from less than nothing, because it seems to have been almost a counter-productive organization when he took over."

Joe readily assented, and following the same line of thought told Mike to add "courage—because it's taken a lot of guts to stand firm against some of the pressures he's had to face."

The three looked at their handiwork so far on the computer screen, and after adding "patience" and "good listener" to the list they decided they had put enough.

"Now we come to the interesting bit," Mike said. "What Bible character are we going to link Bill to?"

Georgina was the first off the mark. "How about Paul? After all, he's made both of you Timothys, and every Timothy needs a Paul."

"True," said Joe, "and he did say he took Paul's visit to Athens as the blueprint for the way he tackled the work here. But somehow it doesn't seem to fit. He's such a doer rather than a thinker. Not that Paul wasn't a man of action too, of course, but I somehow can't picture Bill sitting down and writing an epistle to Fairmont."

"A 'doer,' eh?" mused Mike. "Then how about Joshua—there's a man of action for you. You could say he conquered Fairmont for Christ like Joshua conquered Canaan."

Joe punched his thigh with excitement.

"Yes, that's it, Joshua." Then his eye caught the first word of their description, "faith." "On second thought, how about Joshua's friend, Caleb? Now he really was a man of faith."

Georgina, the peacemaker, rushed to the rescue with an inspired compromise. "Let's make it both of 'em—let's say Bill is Joshua and Caleb rolled into one."

Mike clapped delightedly and immediately tapped in "*J* and *C*."

He had only just finished when the click of the door lock announced Bill had returned. Joe shot out from the little alcove and stood face-to-face confronting the grinning youth pastor.

"William Pulkington, this is your life!"

Then he slapped him on the back and pulled him over.

"Come and meet yourself!" he cried.

Though he wouldn't admit it, Bill was just a mite apprehensive as to what his electronic mirror on the wall would tell him. He didn't expect to be the fairest of all, but he hoped he would not read anything too traumatic.

In the event, he was not a little stunned by the warmth of affection and appreciation the three had transmitted onto the screen.

"Now look, you guys," he protested. "Whoever that fellow is, it's not me. You haven't put one negative thing about me. Now let me get on to that thing and tell you the truth as it really is."

He tried to push Mike off the seat but Joe stopped him, saying, "Oh, we *know* you're not perfect. And you know you're not either—so let's leave it there. We were just going to have fun with your Bible doubles when you came in. Don't spoil it."

For the first time Bill noticed the biblical code letters at the bottom.

"*J* and *C*," he puzzled. "I don't get it."

"It's our turn to be the Bible teachers now," chirped Georgina. "It stands for Joshua and Caleb."

Mike swung around in the computer seat, much in the manner Bill had so many times these few nights. Bill couldn't help thinking of Elijah's mantle falling on Elisha, but made no comment to avoid a digression.

"Right," said Mike, putting on his best Bible teaching tone. "Let's all get our Bibles and let's turn to . . . turn to . . . "

"Numbers 13?" murmured Bill.

"Numbers 13, thank you." Mike accepted the offer gratefully. The apprentice didn't know his Bible quite as well as his mentor yet. He felt he'd better not stick his neck out too far again so he decided to play a safety shot in the form of a question to Bill.

"Do you think this chapter ties up with your experience at all, Bill?"

"I've never really thought along those lines before, I must admit, but as I look down these verses, yes, I do see some coincidences. For example, this reconnaissance expedition the Israelites went on, a man from each tribe. Well it wasn't quite like that, but just as you recently did Mike, I came here and investigated before I accepted the invitation to become youth pastor 10 years ago. I have to say I did not like what I saw. I told you earlier in the evening how the place struck me like a miniature Athens, with people very religious in the wrong way, worshiping the modern idols of materialism and self-interest, while the church in general and the youth group in particular looked a mess.

"Now it so happened that our Bible college president (I was still a student at the time) was Fairmont-born and bred, though he'd gone to a different church, so he reckoned he knew the place inside out. When he head that this opportunity had come up, he had me in his office double quick.

"'Bill,' he said in a fatherly kind of way, 'I know you, I know Fairmont, and I know the church, and I want to tell you as strongly as I can—don't go. That place has been the spiritual graveyard of so many good men, it's a wonder the Lord doesn't put an angel with a flaming sword on the highway to stop any more of His valuable servants going to their doom.'

"He went on to give me a few horror stories of men he knew in different churches here who'd gone bananas with nervous breakdowns or who had been forced out of the ministry and goodness knows what else. He hinted darkly that he thought occult powers might be at work—a claim, incidentally, that I afterwards found to be not without foundation, though that's another story.

"Well, that interview left me in a bit of a turmoil, I can tell you. I sought out others who knew the place to get a different perspective, but whether I was unlucky in my choice of interviewees or not, I don't know. All I do know is the picture seemed to get gloomier and gloomier."

"Perhaps you shouldn't have gone around asking, and just come anyway," said Joe.

"You may well be right," Bill replied. "Looking at this account of the spying expedition in Numbers 13, it gives the impression it was at God's command. But if you look at what Moses says in Deuteronomy 1:22, he puts it down to the people's idea, which suggests that the Lord's directive was only a granting of the people's faithless desire. Perhaps the whole thing was a mistake. Be that as it may, certainly as I got opinion after opinion I found my faith being chipped away."

"But what was God saying to you all this time?" Georgina wanted to know.

"Ah, now that's the interesting thing. When I first had the letter completely out of the blue asking me to go and look at the church, I felt quite a warm attraction, and almost heard a whisper inside saying, 'This is it.' Not that I relied on those subjective feelings, of course. But all my Bible readings seemed very positive, and pointed in the direction of coming. On top of that, on my little sortie here, I had the marvelous privilege of leading someone to the Lord. I was sitting on the park bench at the end of this very street and it just happened. It was so easy. I almost somersaulted into the fishpond with joy."

Mike found that idea of Bill's massive frame doing such an extraordinary thing somewhat incongruous, but he had a more important point to make.

"In a way, that was just like the Israelite reconnaissance party bringing back the fruit of the land," he said.

"That's absolutely the way I saw it, and I think it was that as much as anything else that persuaded me it was the Lord's will I should come. So I accepted the invitation."

Georgina was a little perplexed. "Bill, I remember you did a series with us once on Proverbs, and you talked about wisdom and quoted 11:14, 'Many advisers make victory sure.' You warned us then about ignoring godly advice and charging along our own way, regardless."

Bill smiled. "I'm glad you remember some of the things I say. But I'm not really contradicting myself. The difference in the Fairmont affair was that I wasn't going after a personal whim, but following a deep conviction of what the Lord's will was."

"How do you know the difference?" Joe asked bluntly.

"I believe it is the witness of the Spirit, by which I mean what God is saying to you inside."

Bill noted without surprise that Joe looked far from convinced. "You'll want to know how we can be sure what is the Spirit's voice. Well, first make sure what you plan isn't against any plain command of Scripture. God will never contradict Himself, d'you see. Then ask yourself in all your regular Bible reading, is God speaking to me through this? You'll be amazed how certain passages light up. Mind you, I wouldn't advise opening the Bible at random, though it can't be denied the Lord does sometimes lead His people that way. Circumstances can also be a confirming word, like my experience with the man on the park bench, but I would never rely on circumstances alone. Also, I wouldn't rule out the possibility of a word of prophecy, but that is open to such abuse you need to be as wary as a chipmunk. But in the end, the deciding thing is a certainty deep inside your heart that God has spoken, a fathomless peace. When you've got that, then even though circumstances and people are against you, you will go on because that inner witness becomes a mainspring of your faith."

Mike had been looking over the Bible passage again. He said, "I love the way Caleb expresses his certainty. There's a kind of robust bounciness that can't be squashed. Look at verse 30, how he silences the whole crowd of grumblers—'We should go up and take possession of the land, for we can certainly do it,' and again in chapter 14, verse 9: 'Do not be afraid of the people of the land, because we will swallow them up. Their protection is gone, but the Lord is with us. Do not be afraid of them.' It's great, isn't it?"

"It certainly is," Bill agreed. "And what stands out for me is the way that his tremendous commitment to going into the Promised Land doesn't come from a sort of human determination. You know what I mean: 'We can do it, fellas, come on, follow me.' No, it isn't that at all, but it's 100 percent trust in the Lord, that if He's promised something, He'll do it, whatever the odds. Caleb would certainly subscribe to the old saying, 'One with God is a majority.'"

"That helps me a lot about a problem I've had," said

Georgina. "I hear a lot of Christians down at the church saying, 'I'm trusting the Lord for this, and I'm trusting the Lord for that'—sometimes for really trivial things like a new dress or something, when they're earning quite enough money to go and buy the thing if only they weren't stashing their cash away. Or sometimes they say they're trusting the Lord to get through their exams, and they're out at parties instead of studying. But I see now that what they've got is not faith but presumption."

"You've been very astute to pick that up," responded Bill, another smile crossing his face. "That's bothered me too. No doubt Mike will help set them straight. If you want a biblical example of presumption masquerading as faith you've got one right in front of you in chapter 14, verses 39-45, which, incidentally, also shows how important it is to move in the Lord's timing. Leave it, and it may be too late."

"You know, Bill," Mike said, "you remind me of Gladys Aylward."

"It must be my good looks!" chuckled the very masculine Bill, thrown off balance a bit at the unlikely comparison.

"Uh . . . who's Gladys Aylward?" queried Georgina.

"She was a British missionary who died a few years ago. How Bill—and Caleb for that matter—remind me of her is that she was absolutely convinced God wanted her to go to China. The trouble was, she was an uneducated parlormaid, and the missionary society just didn't think she had it in her. So do you know what she did? She saved up every penny she could until she had enough money—just—for a single train ticket across Europe, Russia, and Asia, and got there under her own steam. In the end she became a heroine for saving hundreds of Chinese children during the Second World War.

"Just suppose she had given in to the people-pressure that said, 'You're not called!' Think what the world would have missed."

"I'm sure I'm not in the same league as Gladys Aylward," the modest Bill said firmly, "but yes, we did share the same problem. And if she is anything like me, she must have had to gulp now and again as she realized what a fool she looked in other people's eyes."

"That takes courage, I guess," said Joe, "which is something I've always admired in you."

Bill would have blushed if he had been the blushing sort. "True, Joe, it does take courage to stand against the crowd. But however tough you might think I look, inside I can be a real jellybaby! We can only keep going if we are sure the Lord is with us because we know it's His power, not ours. If you are really serious about making me an incarnation of Joshua and Caleb, then I'll point you to Joshua 1:9, where the Lord commissions Joshua."

Bill flipped his Bible pages over and read, "'Be strong and courageous. Do not be terrified; do not be discouraged, for the Lord your God will be with you wherever you go.'" He looked up and continued, "Strong as he was, Joshua nevertheless needed to hear those words, and so have I, over and over again. I think it's significant that the Lord spoke them alongside His exhortation to Joshua to study the law. You can only keep up the kind of dare-all faith we've been talking of if you keep yourself immersed in the Word of God."

Joe pointed to the word "perseverance" on the computer screen.

"That's something Mike felt about you, Bill. Do you think it's true?"

"I don't think it's for me to say, Joe. But I think it goes without saying that faith isn't faith unless it does keep going through thick and thin. It was years before I saw real fruit here at Fairmont, as you know, with people like yourselves coming to know the Lord, and maybe sometimes I got a little impatient. But my waiting was nothing to Caleb's. He had this marvelous promise that because he had been faithful he would be one of only two of his contemporaries who would inherit the land of Canaan. And then the poor guy had to go tramping around the desert for 40 years waiting until the go-ahead to get his prize. And the delay was not his fault at all. I think I'd have found that galling.

"However, eventually he got there, and you can't hold the old man down. I mean, there he is, 85 years old and he's so enthusiastic. His particular piece of land is full of warlike people, big, strong, and powerful, and do you see what he says? Look, there in Joshua 14:11 and 12."

Joe was first to find the place, so he read: "'I am still as strong today as the day Moses sent me out; I'm just as vigorous to go out to battle now as I was then. Now give me this hill country that the Lord promised me that day. You yourself heard then that the Anakites were there and their cities were large and fortified, but, the Lord helping me, I will drive them out, just as He said.'"

"What a man he was!" exclaimed Bill admiringly.

"What a youth pastor we've had!" chimed Georgina, mischievously, but meaning it.

"Folks, you do me great honor, and I don't deserve it. But if you really want me to be true-to-type in the mold of Caleb and Joshua, then you must all three promise me one thing."

"OK, what?" Joe voiced the question for them all.

"Pray for me that at the end of my days, it will be possible to write for me the same epitaph Caleb earned. Joshua, chapter 14, verse 14: 'he followed the Lord, the God of Israel, *wholeheartedly*'" (italics added).

And even as he spoke, Mike was tapping out the word "wholehearted" on Bill's file. The accolade was already earned. Epitaph time could wait.

Chapter 13

Bill pulled back the cuff of his sweater and checked his watch.

"Hey, you guys," he cried out. "Do you realize what the time is? It's a quarter after ten! I'm gonna kick you all out 'cause I gotta be up early in the morning."

Bill's experience of youth leadership through many bleary-eyed years had taught him you had to take some kind of strong initiative and cut the courtesy if you ever wanted to get some sleep.

The three young people took no offense, grinned understandingly, and began to make moves to leave the apartment. Bill was standing in front of his computer, ready to shut it down for the night, when suddenly he exclaimed.

"No, hold it! This is the last time I'm going to be able to go through my files with you, Mike, and there's one more I desperately want to show you. Can you stay?"

Mike nodded. "Sure—I've got no wife waiting with a baseball bat."

"You wait," Georgina twinkled, "you haven't met Laura yet."

Mike wouldn't have admitted it, but he was blushing quite pinkly. Georgina carried on speaking. "Can we stay, too? Promise we'll go straight after."

"Will it be OK with your dad?" queried a concerned Bill.

"Oh, sure," said Georgina. "He doesn't try anything like that now."

"Then I guess it's alright."

They all returned to their seats, Mike wondering why one particular file should be so important.

Bill sat facing the screen, which was blank except for a flashing cursor. "This is one of those files I've kept even though the person concerned has now left us. The reason I've kept it is not nostalgia, but because there are some lessons to be learned. I'm afraid, Mike, that I'm going to be ending on a negative note telling you about one of our losers. But if it helps you head off a defeat for someone else, or for yourself for that matter, it will be worth it."

By now thoroughly intrigued, Mike waited for Bill to access the desired data, while Georgina and Joe were looking at each other quizzically, trying to guess which of the Fairmont young people Bill was talking about. But when the information appeared on the screen their puzzlement largely remained. They saw a name they recognized, but knew little about, for the young man had been gone some years and Bill had said very little to Joe about him in all their many times of fellowship. They read:

"Daryl Brown: Age (now) 26. Address: Unknown. Too handsome for his own good; popular, decisive, identifies with people, but very proud. Nurses his grudges, inclined to revenge. Family relationships poor. *Abs*"

Joe expressed his astonishment. "That's from way back. Daryl's been gone seven years or more—before I was old enough to know anything about what was going on. But what's so special about him anyway, apart from having the dad he has?"

"Should I know his dad, then?" asked Mike, pondering if among all the Brown's he knew there might be a famous one who had sired a son called Daryl.

"No, you won't know him," Bill answered. "The special thing about Daryl's dad is that he was the pastor of the church when I arrived—you know, the one who wouldn't take any action over Abe and Cindy."

Bill swivelled his chair 20 degrees to face Joe and said,

"That's why I haven't talked about him with you before, Joe. I felt that I had a duty not to criticize the past ministry of this church in front of our own young people. It would be disloyal. I'm only sharing this file with you now because you will be involved with Mike in the running of this group, helped by the future Mrs. Miller, so all three of you will benefit from what I'm going to tell you, provided you don't let the sordid aspects become objects of unseemly relish."

Georgina had been silent all this time. She stepped into the conversation to ask, "*Abs*—what or who is that, Bill? I've been racking my brains and I can't think."

"Either of you two men know?" Bill looked from one to the other.

Puzzled frowns and a shaking of heads gave a negative answer, but sharp-eyed Georgina had spied one unpacked book, a fat Bible dictionary. She quickly leaned over to reach for it and with even greater rapidity counted the pages of the "*A*'s" until she found what she was looking for.

"Absalom," she announced. "Must be—there is no one else with those first three letters."

Joe was more baffled now. He voiced his bewilderment. "From what I remember of the Absalom story, I can't see how any of that could have happened in Fairmont. At least not so I wouldn't have heard about it, even though I was so young at the time."

"Remember," said Bill, "that my files are more to do with personality types and attitudes than actual duplicating of events. But nevertheless, I do find the whole Daryl affair quite unsavory. The fact you were unaware of it is a tribute to the Christian discretion of people closest to the problem at the time. Actually it seems to me from my reading of the Absalom story that certainly in the beginning even that mess was quite well-hidden, otherwise Amnon wouldn't have survived so long. But I could be wrong because David presumably heard via the palace gossip."

"Amnon?" Mike questioned. "Bill, I hate to admit this, but you've lost me. I'm very hazy over this particular Bible story. I'm not even sure who Absalom was."

"Sorry, Mike," apologized Bill. "Funny, really, how this story is so little known, and yet it's one of the most dramatic in the whole Bible. In fact, I often wonder why someone doesn't make an opera of it. It's got all the ingredients for a Wagnerian blockbuster.

"OK, let's get the low-down on Absalom before we talk about Daryl. In point of fact the story is very, very long, l-o-n-g-e-r than any of Joe's fish that got away."

Bill spread his hands wide as he stretched the syllable in a side-swipe at Joe's passionate hobby.

"So the best thing we can do is make a quick summary. We'll turn to the relevant chapters in the Bible to keep us from going astray, but we won't read them completely. The place we're looking for is 2 Samuel 13-19."

Mike grimaced at the thought of seven Old Testament chapters at this late hour.

"I'll be as brief as I can," Bill promised.

"Absalom was one of David's sons and he had a sister, Tamar. She became the victim of an incestuous rape committed by their half-brother Amnon, who then turned right against her. Absalom bided his time a couple of years before having Amnon murdered, after which he had to flee. Three years later, Joab, David's general, intervened to get David to give into his fatherly feelings and allow Absalom back to Jerusalem. However, the king still would not let his son into the palace until Absalom forced Joab into putting further pressure on David.

"So far you could say that there is a streak of nobility in Absalom, the way he stood up for his sister and so on. But now he does something really sneaky. He starts criticizing the king and his administration to everyone who comes along, and tells them what a better job he would make of things if he were in charge. The culmination of all this is that he gets himself proclaimed king and becomes the leader of a major rebellion. David has to flee for his life out of Jerusalem.

"In the end there is a big battle, and Absalom meets a grisly end, first getting his head caught in the boughs of an oak, and then being speared by Joab and hacked to bits by 10 of Joab's men.

"Though King David has won, he is heartbroken and treats

the victory like a defeat—much to Joab's annoyance, who takes him to task in no uncertain terms. And that's about it. A very tragic end to a very tragic tale. You really must read it through for yourself, Mike. A quick sketch like I've given can't do it anything like fair justice."

Mike nodded an indication that this was his very intention. As it was, glancing at one paragraph and another as Bill had given his summary, had moved him quite a bit. Pathos sighed in almost every comma. But he hadn't forgotten the reason for them looking at this sorry story at almost 11 o'clock at night.

"How does Daryl fit in with all this?" he inquired.

"Let me say at once, lest you're wondering, he wasn't involved in anything as horrid as incestuous rape, though he did get a girl in trouble and he did cause a lot of heartbreak. I'll start at the beginning. In fact, in a way, I'll begin before the beginning, because I think the seeds of what went wrong were there before any actual trouble blew up, and this is a direct parallel with Absalom. What I mean is that David was far too soft as a father, and that was Daryl's dad's problem too. Take David: we have a picture of him as the great all-action, macho hero, killing lions, bears, and giants, and fearless in everything. But inside his own family, things look different. In one way that's good, because he so tender. You read of the way he fasted and prayed when Bathsheba's baby was dying, for example. But on the other hand, it meant there was little or no discipline when it was needed. Amnon rapes Tamar—what does David do? He hears about it, he's furious, but he does nothing (2 Sam. 13:21). That seems totally inconceivable, doesn't it? Then again, Absalom kills Amnon, he flees, the king is upset and mourns for his son every day (see verse 37), but again he does nothing. Even when Absalom comes back, David keeps him at a distance instead of getting the thing resolved once for all. It's a fact you'll learn as you start to carry out your work in leadership, Mike, that people would rather be admonished and disciplined than ignored. But we all flunk confrontation—I have, so many times. But buying peace that way gets you some dud bargains, I assure you.

"That's how it was with David, and that's how it was with Daryl's dad. He doted on Daryl, and it wasn't that he couldn't see any wrong in him. He just hoped if he said nothing, everything would work out alright.

"The effect was that Daryl grew up believing he could get away with anything. He had a somewhat inflated idea of his own ability anyway, and like I say on the file, he was too handsome for his own good. So by the time he got to his early teens he was living quite unlike the child of the parsonage. He used his looks and his popularity to draw his own circle of friends, and lived his own life independent of home and church."

"Good for him," Mike said unexpectedly.

The others stared incredulously.

He thought he'd better explain. "I hate the stereotype of the minister's son," he blushed. "You see, I'm one myself, and I know all about the pressures. Everyone expecting you to be goodie-goodie. It's awful."

Bill gently corrected him. "I can understand your frustration, and I'm certainly not one to turn the moral screw on a kid just because he happened to be born in a pile of sermon notes. But Daryl wasn't just a PK in understandable revolt. There was a growing cynicism in him about the whole church setup. I think he had a real chip on his shoulder."

"Why?" fired Georgina.

"Because this glossing over of his misdoings got interpreted by him as rejection—the last thing Daryl's father ever intended. You see, by ignoring the multitude of minor sins and transgressions, which themselves may partly have been cries for help, Daryl's dad made his son feel he wasn't important. Add to that what all preacher's kids have to put up with, namely the time problem of their pop always being at the church or in somebody else's house, or having somebody visit them, and you can see what a chunk of a chip Daryl carried."

Joe interrupted Bill's flow, pointing to his Bible. "I can see the link with Absalom here," he said. "Look, verses 22 and 23 of chapter 13. It tells us Absalom waited two years for his revenge, all that time not speaking anything good or bad of Amnon. Boy, what a time to carry a grudge! He must really have been smoldering!"

"That's nothing," smiled the experienced Bill. "I've known

some people to carry grudges for decades and take them with them to their graves. If only people would learn the truth of Ephesians 4:26, 'Do not let the sun go down while you are still angry,' what a lot of trouble and distress the world would have been saved. But I'm digressing. Yes, Joe, of course you're right, and I think this trait of bearing a grudge, letting resentment burn like a tortuously slow fuse until it ignites a devastating vengeful explosion, was with Absalom right through his life. That, I believe, is the explanation of how he could bring himself to plot against his father David. I think he resented not only David's non-handling of the original rape, but also David's procrastination in bringing him back. It's awful to be that way.

"Unfortunately there is something else that made Absalom even worse, and it is something he has in common with Daryl. I mean our old arch-enemy No. 1: pride."

"Like Saul and Corky?" suggested Mike.

"Exactly," Bill affirmed, "only more so. You may remember I said that Saul and Corky had some modesty. Daryl and Absalom had none. Absalom seemed to believe he was the answer to everyone's prayer. Gifted with a handsome face, crowned by hair that was the admiration of all the haute coiffeur hairdressers of Israel, he didn't see why he shouldn't be king. Undoubtedly that pride and his low estimation of his father fed each other so that both grew to the gigantic proportions that pushed him into rebellion.

"Coming back to Daryl. I think one of the most hurtful things he was doing at this time was sniping at his father behind his back. For example, when I arrived 10 years ago and he was a 16-year-old, I found it sickening to hear the kind of cheap jokes he would make at his dad's expense. I'm all for good banter myself, and the man of God who can't take a laugh against himself won't last very long. But these were sour quips, nasty solar-plexus punches."

Mike wanted an example.

"Well, one that comes to mind is when we were studying 1 Corinthians and I read out the verse, 'God chose the foolish things of this world,' he said, 'That explains it!' I said, 'Explains what?' and he said, 'Why my dad's a minister!' That was pretty cheap, but he got his laugh.

"Well, at this time, he was living a kind of loose life-style: lots of parties, lots of girls. I suspect some drug involvement too. And so the inevitable happened. He got a girl pregnant. Put it down to luck, the Lord's graciousness to his dad, or whatever, but this particular girl wasn't from Fairmont, she was from upstate. That made it possible for everything to be hushed up. I'm not convinced that was the best thing to do, but that's what happened and it was right in character with Pastor Brown's low-profile approach to everything. He took me into his confidence, though, which I really appreciated, and that's how I know the details.

"I'll never forget that time he told me. He was a broken man. But I have to say this. A lot of the criticism that I've been making of him in this last hour is from his own self-analysis that he poured out to me in that interview. He had been doing an awful lot of praying and thinking since his son, as blasé as ever, had broken the news to him. The danger then was that Pastor Brown would be so self-condemning and guilt-ridden over his performance as a father that he would be paralyzed from doing anything. But his wife was a tower of strength and together they got a plan of action, which involved, among other things, their son taking up his full responsibilities towards the girl and her child, though without marrying her, for there was no real love match there. They made sure Daryl took care of all the hospital bills, made proper contact with the girl's parents and apologized to them, and so on.

"There's no doubt there was a new firmness about our pastor's whole ministry from that time on, and the year that remained before he retired was the most fruitful the church had ever experienced. As for his son, well, although he was resentful at first, he began to respect his dad's new approach. He was beyond the age when spanking was an option in his father's repertoire of correction, but he submitted to his father's sheer words, because of the authority and love behind them. The resentment went, the pride was humbled, and last I heard they have a great relationship. I see them about every year or so; in fact, I'll be visiting them in about three months' time."

Georgina loved happy endings and the relief on her face was plain. But she couldn't forget the much less happy ending of Absalom. She was looking down in her Bible at David's heartfelt cry following his son's death. "O my son Absalom! My son, my son Absalom! If only I had died instead of you—O Absalom, my son, my son!" (2 Sam. 18:33).

She pointed the verse out to Bill.

"That breaks my heart," she said. "It seems such a tragic waste of life."

"That's what happens when God's laws are broken. And the Lord's people aren't immune from His judgment. But doesn't that verse give you some hope too, Georgina?"

"In what way?" she asked.

"I think I know," Joe said. "We are God's children who've gone astray from Him as much as Absalom did from David."

Mike took over, cottoning on to the line of thought.

"I get it! The Lord weeps over us too, but the difference from David is that He *has* died instead of us, so we can be forgiven and we can start again."

"That's it," Bill smiled, his face spontaneously creating a dozen new laughter lines.

"And that's why I wanted you to stay for this last file of mine, even though at first sight it looked like a loser. I want my last word to be that there is always hope for the losers to become winners. Watch!"

His fingers pressed a different key from before, calling up a print command buried in his complex program. A large cross filled one half of the screen and beside it a text.

"God demonstrates his own love for us in this:
While we were still sinners, Christ died for us.
Romans 5:8."

He touched the key again. The cross was replaced by a silhouette figure with outstretched hands and the text changed to read:

> "We implore you on Christ's behalf: Be reconciled to God. God made him who had no sin to be sin for us, so that in him we might become the righteousness of God. 2 Corinthians 5:20,21."

A third touch on the key and the picture changed yet again. This time a rising sun, rays reaching out in a 180-degree arc, had superimposed on it the words:

> "Giving thanks to the Father, who has qualified you to share in the inheritance of the saints in the kingdom of light. For he has rescued us from the dominion of darkness and brought us into the kingdom of the Son he loves, in whom we have redemption, the forgiveness of sins. Colossians 1:12-14."

"Those are the verses that show me there is hope for our losers to become winners. The door is open, if only they'll walk through it.

"Anyway, that's it—time for bed. I'll print out all those files for you tomorrow, Mike, so you can have a permanent record."

Mike was looking thoughtful. "Thanks, Bill, I'd appreciate that," he said. "But is it possible to have a copy of the disks too? It could just be I'll be making a visit to the computer shop tomorrow."